Curious Histories of Provence

Curious Histories of Provence

Tales from the South of France

Margo Lestz

ISBN: 978-0-9931371-6-7

Published by
Boo-Tickety Publishing
London

Contents

PROVENCE

Introduction

Stories and Histories...

What better way to really understand a region than by learning its history and listening to its stories?

In this book, I'll share with you some of the intriguing tales that I've discovered about that magical place known as Provence. From cicadas to dragons, and Nostradamus to Buffalo Bill, this book is filled with informative and entertaining stories about the south of France.

I hope you'll enjoy perusing them as much as I've enjoyed finding and writing about them.

Happy Reading!

PART 1:
ESSENTIAL
PROVENCE

After God had created the earth, sun, mountains and sea, he found himself with a handful of leftovers. What could he do with all these beautiful remnants? He didn't want to waste them, so he decided to make his own personal paradise. And this is how Provence came to be.

– A Provençal legend

Lavender

Wake Up and Smell the Lavender

Rows of fragrant lavender plants stretching toward the horizon are an unforgettable sight. In fact, for many people, this is the first image that comes to mind when they think of Provence. You might imagine that the landscape has always been swathed in lines of lavender, but you would be wrong. Growing the purple plant in this fashion only began in the twentieth century.

Since time immemorial, wild lavender, called *lavande*, has dotted Provence's rocky hilltops where shepherds and local peasants gathered it for their personal use. But when the University of Montpellier began to research lavender's medicinal uses in the eighteenth century, demand for the aromatic herb rose. Crews of women and children, armed with cloth bags, departed daily to wander around the mountaintops gathering flowers from wild lavender plants. It was a time-consuming and inefficient method of harvesting.

When the perfumeries of Grasse expanded at the end of the nineteenth century, the demand increased even more, and lavender began to be treated as a crop. A hybrid, called *lavandin,* was developed which could be cultivated at a lower altitude. But there were no long purple rows in sight, as *lavandin* was planted in squares with space around each plant to make room for the harvesters. It still had to be harvested by hand, but at least the women and children no longer had to hike up the mountains to find it.

In 1950 the harvesting machine was invented, and this changed everything. The landscape was transformed into the now-familiar lines of lavender with space between each row for the mechanical picker.

Well, that's the traditional version of why we see long rows of purple lavender in Provence today. But, of course, there is a legend...

How Lavender Came to be
Cultivated in Provence
A Legend

Once upon a time, there was a small, blue-eyed fairy called Lavendula. She was born high on a mountain in the Alpes-de-Haute-Provence where the wild lavender grows, and she lived there her entire life. It was certainly beautiful, but Lavendula started to get "itchy feet." She yearned to see more of the world, so she came down from her high perch to visit the plains of Provence.

When Lavendula saw the dry, barren fields scorched by the unrelenting sun, her tender heart was saddened, and she began to cry. The tears from her blue eyes rolled down her cheeks and landed on the soil, making puddles of violet-blue water. She cried so much that she ended up standing in a small pond.

When she finally pulled herself together and saw what she had done, she tried to wipe up the blue tears. But the more she wiped, the more the color spread in long swaths across the land. Soon, blue-violet lines were everywhere, and out of this grew the long rows of lavender that have become one of the most recognized symbols of Provence.

Legend of the Four Thieves

As well as being beautiful and smelling divine, lavender has been appreciated for its many uses since antiquity: scenting cosmetics and perfumes, cleaning and sanitizing laundry, adding flavor to foods, aiding relaxation, driving away insects, and healing maladies.

But in the 1700s, a brazen band of burglars near Marseille found another use for it. At that time, there was a plague in the land, and people were dropping like flies. The pestilence had everyone in the city shaking in their shoes. No one dared to go into, or even near, a home where the ultra-contagious disease had struck.

However, there was a gang of four bold bandits who would creep into the infected houses and steal anything and everything of value. They even dug through the pockets of the dead. The villagers were shocked. Who would dare to rob the dead and dying? And, maybe even more importantly, why didn't they fall sick themselves? Everyone was desperate to find these criminals and learn their secret for avoiding the plague.

The law finally caught up with the four thieves, and they were offered a deal: if they revealed their secret plague protection, the judge would go easy on them and they wouldn't be hanged. The robbers, being fond of their necks, told all. They handed over their recipe for a special herbal concoction made with vinegar-soaked plants – and lavender was one of the main ingredients. They had rubbed this herbal vinegar all over themselves every day. It had protected them from the disease and allowed them to carry on their burgling duties without taking a single sick-day.

The herbal plague protection formula was posted all over Marseille and saved many lives. This antiseptic liquid became known as *Vinaigre des Quatre Voleurs* (Vinegar of the Four Thieves). It was registered in the Codex of Medicines in 1748 and was sold in pharmacies as an antiseptic for hundreds of years. In fact, with a bit of searching, it can still be found today. There are several variations to the recipe and in most of them, lavender is still a key ingredient.

Lavender and the Origins of Aromatherapy

The word "aromatherapy" was coined by a man who spent most of his life working with lavender. In fact, lavender even saved his life.

René-Maurice Gattefossé was a French chemical engineer who worked for his family's cosmetic company. In the early 1900s, he began experimenting with essential oils, and took a special interest in lavender. He felt confident these plant oils contained healing properties.

Then, one day in 1910, when tragedy struck, he put them to the test. While Monsieur Gattefossé was working in the lab, there was an explosion. Both his hands were badly burned and developed gas gangrene (a fast-spreading and deadly condition). They were getting worse by the day, so he doused them with lavender oil. After just one rinse of the oil, the gangrene stopped spreading and the tissue began to heal.

This confirmed Monsieur Gattefossé's research and made him a true believer in the healing properties of essential oils. He continued his experiments, and during World War I he consulted with doctors about the use of these oils to treat soldiers' wounds and to disinfect hospitals.

Through his work Gattefossé met lavender growers who were barely able to make a living during the early 1900s. Taking their plight to heart, he began holding conferences to advise them on how to better organize their farms and distilleries to be more profitable. Later in life, Gattefossé even became a bit of a lavender farmer himself. In 1940 he bought a Provençal *mas* (farmhouse) called *Mas Bellile* in Saint-Rémy-de-Provence. There he grew lavender (and other plants) and distilled their essential oils for his research.

The word "aromatherapy" comes from a book Gattefossé published in 1937. The French title was *Aromathérapie: Les Huiles Essentielles – Hormones Végétales*, but the English version was simply called *Aromatherapy*. While the term "aromatherapy" may have originated with Monsieur Gattefossé, the idea of plant oils containing beneficial properties existed long before him and is still alive and well today.

Types of Lavender

All lavender is not created equal. There are three types of lavender growing in Provence:

Lavande is the fine or true lavender which grows above 700 meters. Its essential oils are used in perfume and medicine.

Aspic grows lower but has a strong camphoric odor. It's often blended with *lavande* for medicinal uses.

Lavandin is a hybrid lavender that can grow below 600 meters. This is the lavender you will see growing in those long purple rows. It makes up 90% of the lavender grown in Provence and is used in soaps and cosmetics.

What to See and Do

Route de la Lavande
There are several driving (or biking) routes that will lead you through the lavender fields. You will find museums along the way where you can learn all about growing and distilling lavender. And, of course, you will pass a multitude of shops where you can buy any number of products made with lavender: honey, perfume, soaps... This site has a variety of lavender route maps:
http://www.moveyouralps.com/en/routes-de-la-lavande

Lavender Festival
The *Corso de la Lavande* in Digne-les-Bains is the best-known lavender festival, featuring a parade with lavender floats during the first weekend in August.

- Lavender can bloom from around the end of June to the beginning of August – it all depends on weather conditions. It's advisable to call the local tourist office for an estimate of the best time and location to see the blooms.

The Cicada
(La Cigale)

The Sun Makes Them Sing

When the warm days of summer arrive in Provence, the air is filled with the song of the cicadas, or *cigales* in French. They're the loudest insects on the planet and their "song" has been measured at up to 120 decibels – comparable to a motorcycle.

The male cicada produces that characteristic chirping sound by rapidly contracting a special membrane in his abdomen. This noise – or song, for those more poetically inclined – is a mating call. However, *Monsieur Cigale* can only serenade the ladies when the temperature is about 25°C (77°F) or higher because at lower temperatures, his noise-making membrane loses its elasticity.

So, when the temperature rises and all those male cicadas get heated up and start crooning, Provence can get pretty noisy. With so much racket going on during the hottest part of the day, you might wonder how the good Provençal folk are able to enjoy their long midday siestas. Well, according to legend, the cicadas may have been sent to this area just for the purpose of shortening those afternoon naps.

Why Cicadas Came to Provence
A Legend

A very long time ago, when such things were normal occurrences, two angels decided to spend their summer holiday in Provence. As they packed their bags, visions of an earthly paradise filled their thoughts. However, when they arrived on a warm afternoon, they were shocked to find empty streets, untended gardens, and buildings in need of repair. What could have happened?

They went in search of the priest, hoping he could shed some light on this sad state of affairs. When they found him, he was sound asleep, snoring away on a little cot, under an olive tree behind the church. They gently shook him awake and asked him why the town had fallen into such disrepair. Wiping the sleep from his eyes, the priest replied that Provence had been blessed with so much sunshine, it was just too hot to do any work in the afternoons – so everyone took a nap. Their siestas lasted for hours, and when they awoke, it was time for dinner. After that, it was too late to work.

The angels weren't very happy about this and hurried back to heaven to tattle on the people of Provence. God listened attentively with a slight smile on his lips. He replied, "Don't worry, I have a plan. And I'm just about ready to put it into action. I've created a little insect called the cicada. It will climb into the trees in summer, and the hotter it gets, the louder it will sing. There's no way those sleepy-headed Provençal folks will be able to doze away the afternoon."

The Almighty smiled in self-satisfaction as he blew a cloud of cicadas down to earth and watched them take up their places in the trees. It seemed like the perfect plan. However, the sun was so hot that the people of Provence still fell asleep after lunch. The noise of the cicada, which was meant to keep them awake, sounded like a soothing lullaby to them. So, as it turns out, it's only the visitors to Provence who are disturbed by the cicadas' song.

Il ne fait pas bon de travailler quand la cigale chante.

It's not good to work when the cicada is singing.

– Provençal saying

Symbol of Provence

Instead of regarding the cicada as a pest, the people of Provence adopted the noisy critter as their mascot. The insect became the symbol of Provence thanks to Frédéric Mistral (no relation to the wind of the same name). In 1854, he was one of the founders of the Félibrige, a group of seven poets who worked to restore the Provençal language and keep local culture and history alive. This organization adopted the cicada as their symbol, and Mistral decorated his bookplate with a golden cicada on a blue background with the words *Lou Souleu Mi Fa Canta* (Provençal for "The Sun Makes Me Sing").

Louis Sicard, a ceramicist in Aubagne, took his inspiration from the Félibrige in 1895 when a tile company asked him to design a gift symbolizing Provence. Sicard created a ceramic paperweight in the form of a cicada sitting on an olive branch, bearing the same words Mistral had used: "The Sun Makes Me Sing." The company gave these as gifts to all their clients and Sicard went on to make different variations and sizes of the ceramic cicada. Soon other artisans followed suit, and now they can be found in almost all Provençal markets. They are regarded as good luck charms, and they seem to burrow their way into many a tourist's suitcase.

Cicada in Fable

La Cigale et la Fourmi
or The Grasshopper and the Ant

Long before the cicada became the symbol of Provence, it was a symbol of a carefree attitude toward life in general and specifically toward money. Most English-speakers have heard Aesop's fable about the grasshopper and the ant, but in the original Greek, as in the French version, the grasshopper character is a cicada. In France, the fable was retold by Jean de la Fontaine in the 1600s and is still memorized by all French schoolchildren.

In the fable, Mrs. Cicada sings and enjoys herself all summer long while Mrs. Ant busily stores up food for the coming winter. When the cold weather arrives, the cicada is hungry and goes to her neighbor, the ant, begging for a bit of grain to eat. But the ant refuses, telling Mrs. Cicada that she wasted her time singing all summer, so now maybe she should try dancing. (Ouch!)

This little fable may entertain children and even teach some moral lessons, but obviously, neither Aesop nor Jean de la Fontaine knew much about cicadas. First of all, the cicada who sang all summer long in the fable is female. I'm sure this is because the word *cigale* in French is feminine, but in real life only male cicadas can "sing." Secondly, cicadas die at the end of summer, so Mrs. Cicada wouldn't have been hungry – she would have been dead. But even if she hadn't died, she surely would not have asked the ant for grain, since cicadas live solely on plant sap.

Although the fable isn't entomologically correct, it still causes the French to reflect on whether it's better to be like the cicada and enjoy life without planning for tomorrow, or whether the ant got it right by continuously working and preparing for the future. Some say the cicada's carefree attitude mirrors that of the people of Provence.

Two expressions come from this fable:

- *Etre fourmi* (to be the ant) means to be hardworking and thrifty.
- *Etre cigale* (to be the cicada) means to be a spendthrift.

La Cigale (Cicada)   La Fourmi (Ant)

Life Cycle of a Cicada

The cicada's life above ground is very short, so even though they might seem to be carefree, they are actually on a mission with a deadline. The males get on with their singing, which, if you believe the legend, has two purposes: first to keep the people of Provence from over-napping, and second, to attract females so they can make baby cicadas who will also try to keep the people of Provence from over-napping.

The females, who have been wooed by the music, are busy laying their eggs. They make a slit in the stem of a plant and fill it with 300–400 eggs, of which only about 5% will hatch. When the weather starts to cool, the adults die, but the cycle of life continues when the little larvae hatch and pop their heads out of the plant stem. They either crawl or fall to the ground, and burrow into the soil, where they will spend most of their life as grubs.

After four to six years underground (depending on the species) the little grubs start to make their way to the surface. It seems that after God blew down that first handful of cicadas, he must have done the same thing the following four to six years, because every year there is a new batch popping out of the ground. Near the end of June, when the weather warms up, they emerge and climb into the trees to begin their three or four months of life in the Provençal sun. Once in the trees, they firmly anchor their legs in the bark and then break out of their outer skin, leaving hollow shells attached to the trees. After drying off for a few hours in the warm sunshine, they start up their shift and begin singing. And so, the cycle continues with a new batch of cicadas doing their best to keep those pesky Provençal siestas to a minimum.

Cypress Trees

Secret Language of Cypress Trees

Slender, conical cypress trees are everywhere in Provence: they line roads, outline fields, decorate cemeteries, and adorn houses. These sturdy, practical trees protect crops and homes from the fierce Mistral wind that whips through this area, but there is more to them than meets the eye. It seems these ubiquitous trees may have a hidden meaning depending on where and how they are planted. Let's investigate the secret language of the cypress.

In Cemeteries

Since ancient times, the cypress has been a symbol of eternal life: it stays green year-round, its wood is resistant to decay, it's always bearing fruit, it's fire resistant, and its shape seems to point toward the heavens. For these reasons, it is often planted in cemeteries. In days gone by, a solitary tree would be planted to represent a child, and two trees for a couple. The expression, *Dormir sous un cyprès*, or "to sleep under a cypress" means to be dead.

Around the House

On a happier note, Provençal farmhouses (called *mas*) often have three cypress trees, planted in a triangular shape near the entry to the property. Traditionally, this is a symbol of hospitality. When long-ago travelers passed by and saw three trees, they knew they could rest their weary bones there for the night. Two trees, and they could fill their belly and wet their whistle. But if there was only one tree, it meant "don't even think about stopping here."

Since this is a very old tradition, many people may not be aware of it. So it's probably best not to stop at a house with three cypresses and ask for a meal and a bed – unless you are very well acquainted with the owners.

Good Luck Charm

Another "old tradition," which is actually a new one, declares that cypress trees near a Provençal *mas* bring good luck. This legend conveniently took root in the 1980s, when it was becoming fashionable for Parisians to have a second home in Provence. They would arrive keen to buy a property, but when they spotted cypress trees near the door of their prospective holiday home, they would be reminded of cemeteries and get cold feet.

That wasn't good for the real estate market, so the *notaires* (who supervise real estate transactions in France) and the Office of Tourism got together and invented the "old Provençal tradition" that cypress trees near the entry of a home bring good luck. That made the Parisians feel better and they snapped up those "lucky" farmhouses.

Practicality

There is one more thought about why these trees are planted by farmhouse entrances, and it's a very practical one. Some say that if you plant a few cypress trees when the house is built, you will have replacement beams at hand should one of the originals ever rot or break.

Well, that's all very sensible, but it really muddles things up. For example, if you see a house with only one tree, it could be that the occupants don't want any visitors. Or it could be that they love company, but they just had to replace a beam in their house. What do you do? Do you poke around to see if you can find a stump, or do you keep going? The choice is entirely yours.

The Cypress Code

| Welcome - Have a meal and spend the night. | Welcome - Have a meal then be on your way. | Don't even think about it ! |

The Mistral Wind

Hold On to Your Hat

"*Ce sacré Mistral!*" ("That blessed, or damned, Mistral!") That's what the locals call the strong, cold, dry wind that roars down the Rhone Valley from Lyon to Marseille. Provence claims 32 different winds, but the Mistral is master of them all. The name "Mistral" means masterly in the Provençal language, and according to local expressions, that Master Wind can blow the tail off a donkey or the horns off a bull. However, this powerful wind doesn't just snatch away donkey tails and bull horns: it will also make off with roof tiles, patio furniture, laundry, shallow-rooted trees, flowerpots, rubbish bins, hats, sunglasses... basically anything that isn't tied down.

Some say that once the Mistral starts to blow, it will continue for three, six, or nine days. During this time, people and animals try to stay indoors, but they can't escape the wind's effects. When it's howling outside, pets are said to misbehave more than usual, and people blame the wind's unrelenting roar for causing headaches, making them cranky, and leaving them sleepless. It's even said to drive people mad – *le vent qui rend fou*. One bit of folklore says that once upon a time those who committed a crime while under the maddening influence of the Mistral would have gotten a lighter sentence because of it.

With all these negative effects, you might be confused to find that the people of Provence are actually rather fond of their Master Wind. Even though it might drive them crazy for three, six, or nine days, it's actually quite beneficial to life in Provence. It's thanks, in great part, to this wind that the area sees so much sunshine. The wind blows away the clouds and pollution, leaving behind bright blue skies and fresh air. It also dries up any mildew-creating moisture on the grape vines, keeping them healthy for producing those Provençal wines.

It's the Mistral! Look out for those bull horns and donkey tails!

The Mistral in Legend

An ancient legend explains the love/hate relationship that the people of Provence have with their Master Wind. According to the story, the Mistral's birthplace is the center of the marsh of Vivarais, to the north of the Ardèche, where it comes swooshing through an arched opening in a giant rock.

Many years ago, the people of the windblown cities and towns in the Mistral's path were tired of having the roof tiles ripped off their houses and their laundry scattered across the countryside. They had simply had enough and decided to do something about it. They sent a delegation of brave young men up to the source of the terrible wind to stop it. They built a huge door, big enough to cover the arch where the wind was thought to originate. It was made of the strongest wood and reinforced with iron beams. It would surely hold back the wind.

When they arrived with their colossal door, one man sneaked up to the arch and peeked around. All was quiet, as the wind was taking his afternoon nap. The men moved the huge door over the archway quick as a wink and started to hammer it into place. By the time the wind realized what was happening, it was too late. He was a prisoner.

He howled and rumbled and tried to blow his way through the door, but it was too strong. Then he started to yell at the men on the other side of the door: "When I get out of here, I'm going to blow away everything. I'll make your life miserable!"

"That's what you've been doing," the men replied, "and that's exactly why you're not getting out."

The wind threatened, "You'll be sorry, I'll curse you and all the people of your towns. I'll curse your crops, and I'll curse your animals."

The men nervously checked the beams across the door one more time and left, satisfied that they had done their job well.

The people of the Rhone Valley enjoyed a wonderfully calm winter without that troublesome wind. But when summer rolled around, it brought some unexpected problems. The area was naturally marshy and humid, and without the wind to dry it out, things began to mold, and stagnant water became a breeding ground for insects. The environment became unhealthy, people started to get sick, and the sun was unbearably hot without the Mistral's cooling breeze.

Life grew intolerable and something had to be done. The mayors of the affected towns held a meeting to find a solution to their problem. After much discussion, they all agreed that there was only one option – they had to release the Mistral. It had been more beneficial than they'd realized, and living without it was worse than living with it.

The mayors drew lots to see who would take up the task of freeing the mighty wind. A town close to the sealed-up arch drew the short straw, and a delegation was sent to open the door. When they arrived, the Mistral, who had already gotten wind of the meeting, was waiting for them.

"We want to let you out," the men started, "but we want you to give us your word not to cause all the havoc that you did before."

In a calm voice, the wind said, "I've learned my lesson. If you let me out, I promise to behave, I won't uproot your trees or tear down your fences or blow your roofs off. I'm truly sorry for any problems I caused you. I just didn't know my own strength. You have my word of honor as master of the winds that I'll behave from now on."

The men were relieved and started to take off the door. When they had removed about half the nails, the Mistral broke through with a mighty gust. He zoomed past the startled men, blowing their hats off, then circled back in a rage with a rumbling, roaring noise.

One brave soul found his voice and shouted up at the violent wind, "But you gave us your word – are you a wind whose word means nothing?"

When the Mistral heard this, he felt ashamed of himself and calmed down. He swirled gently around the trees, rustling their leaves, blew the dead leaves off the roofs, softly brushed across the lavender fields, and promised again to tame his infamous temper. The men were satisfied and went home to give the others the happy news.

As the Mistral moved south along the valley in his new milder manner, he realized something: he had only promised the nearby town that he would behave. So, the further he went, the harder he blew. He felt free and happy to be able to knock things over and show off his power.

Even though the Mistral continues to cause mischief and make life difficult for the people of Provence, they have never since tried to contain him. As with any friend, they have learned to accept the wind's faults, enjoy the benefits he brings, and be thankful for his presence in their life.

It's said that this legend was so ingrained in the culture that only 100 or so years ago, the people from the southern villages, who had heard and believed this tale, actually sent a delegation to Viviers where the Mistral is said to originate. They asked the mayor to please open the door for the Mistral a bit less often.

The Mistral You Can See

Although the Mistral itself is invisible, you can see its effects in the Provençal landscape. After thousands of years of living with this wind, whose gusts can exceed 90 kilometers per hour (56 mph), people have learned how to adapt to it.

Houses are built of thick stone with as few windows as possible on the north side, and they have wooden shutters that can be closed tight to protect the glass from flying debris. Roofs are covered with terracotta tiles, sometimes two or three layers thick, which are cemented into place. And sometimes, heavy rocks are placed at the ends of the tiles to give them an extra bit of wind-resistance.

In the towns, narrow streets usually curve to prevent them from becoming wind tunnels, and bell towers are built with open iron framework at the top so the wind can pass through without causing damage.

In the countryside, fields are lined with rows of cypress and poplar trees which keep crops from being blown over and protect the soil from erosion. Many trees have a visible lean toward the south from all the years of being blown in that direction.

Painting the Wind

Vincent Van Gogh, the Dutch post-impressionist painter, spent his last few years in the south of France where he painted some of his most famous works of sunflowers, waving fields of grain, and cypress trees. He moved to Arles in 1888 where he was inspired by the pure light and colors that shone through after the Mistral had blown the clouds away.

But even when the Mistral was raging, Van Gogh was determined to paint. He would drive iron pegs into the ground and tie the legs of his easel to them to keep it from blowing away. Then he had to tie down the canvas – what determination.

It's a well-known fact that Van Gogh had mental problems, and moving to a place with a *vent qui rend fou* ("a wind that drives you mad") probably wasn't the best move for him. In 1889, after the "ear incident" he committed himself to an asylum in St. Remy de Provence where he continued to paint between his bouts of depression.

It was in St. Remy that he completed one of his most recognized works, *The Starry Night*. When you look at this painting and see the swirls in the sky and the swaying cypress trees, you can't help but wonder whether Van Gogh was actually painting the howling Mistral wind.

The original title might have been
"Windy Night"

Mistral Expressions

The Mistral has a great impact on those living in Provence and has several expressions associated with it. Here are a few:

- A wind to tear off a donkey's tail – *un vent à arracher la queue aux ânes.*
- A wind to blow the horns off a bull – *un vent à décorner les boeufs.*
- The wind that drives you mad – *le vent qui rend fou.*
- When it starts to blow on a Monday, it will last three days or one, when it starts to blow on a Thursday, it will last three days or nine – *quand il se leve le lundi, il dure trois jours ou un: quand il se leve le jeudi, il dure trois jours ou neuf.*
- The Mistral is counted as one of the three scourges of Provence. The Mistral takes first place, followed by the Parlement, which was the government seat in Aix from 1486 through the Revolution, and third is the Durance, a river known for its massive flooding when the snow melts in the mountains. *Mistral, Parlement et Durance sont les trois fléaux de Provence.*
- Because of the Mistral's health benefits: When the mistral comes in through the window, the doctor leaves by the door. *Quand le mistral entre par la fenêtre, le médecin sort par la porte.*
- Because the Mistral dries up the marshes and stagnant water, it's called mud-eater – *mange boue* in French and *mango fango* in Provençal.

Red Hills of Roussillon

There is a place in Provence, around the tiny town of Roussillon, where the hills are red. Could they have been burned by the fire of the gods or were they soaked with blood?

Today, we are pretty sure the red hue is due to an abundance of iron oxide in the soil, but before people understood this explanation, they concocted tales to explain the strangely colored hills. One such story is the legend of the Titans...

Legend of the Titans

A very long time ago, the Titans, those giant, mythological Greek gods, set their sights on Provence and wanted the region for themselves. However, the Provençal folk weren't about to give up their beloved land, and a mighty battle ensued. The gods threw down thunderbolts, but the mortals dodged them and pelted the deities with rocks.

This really annoyed the Titans, and they gathered in a cave in the Mont de Vaucluse and built a huge fire cannon. They used it to shoot flames over the hills and burn everything in sight. But the singed populace took shelter in the caverns and, as soon as the earth had cooled a bit, they came right back out and resumed their stone throwing. The rocks thrown by the Provençal folks couldn't hurt the gods, but they annoyed them so much that they finally left. The men, women, and children of Provence proudly claimed their scorched land which has remained red to this day from the fire of the Titans.

Tragic Tale of Seremonda

Another story explaining the color of the hills comes to us from the Middle Ages. (It's a bit gory, so sensitive souls should proceed with caution.)

During medieval times, Seigneur Raimon and his wife, Dame Seremonda, lived in their castle on top of a hill near Roussillon. Every day Raimon would leave his wife alone in the big, cold castle while he went off on hunting trips. Day after day, Seremonda was alone. She would do some needlework or a bit of painting to assuage her boredom before sitting down alone to her evening meal in the cavernous dining room.

One day a troubadour happened to be passing by and knocked on the heavy wooden door. His name was Guillem de Cabestany. He was young, easy on the eye, and he entertained the lady of the château by singing his poems. They were filled with chivalrous stories of knights fighting battles for the honor of their cherished ladies. He sang words of love and respect, words Seremonda had never heard from her husband.

Guillem, being a true gentleman, saw a sad lady before him, and felt it was his duty to lighten her heart with song. So, he came back the next day, and the day after, and the day after... Soon the abandoned wife and the gallant troubadour fell in love and Guillem had succeeded in lifting her sorrow.

However, one of the servants tipped off Raimon that there was an affair afoot. Even though he wasn't interested in spending any time with his wife, Raimon certainly didn't want anyone else to be with her. He devised an evil plan. He invited the young troubadour to go hunting with him. (Warning! Stop reading here if you are squeamish.) He stabbed young Guillem and cut off his head, then cut out his heart. He rode nonchalantly back to the castle with his trophies. He took the heart to the kitchen and instructed his cook to prepare it in a tasty sauce for that evening's dinner. He tucked the head into a basket next to his chair in the great dining hall.

Seremonda was pleasantly surprised that her husband had decided to dine with her that evening and hoped his attitude toward her was changing. They enjoyed an agreeable meal and she even remarked on the delicious food.

After dinner, however, the evil Raimon revealed to Seremonda that she had just eaten the heart of her lover. He opened the basket and pulled out Guillem's severed head as proof. The poor Seremonda went white and nearly fainted. But she composed herself and declared that since she had eaten such a perfect meal, she would never eat again. She walked up to the highest tower of the castle and plunged to her death. Her blood covered the ground and seeped deep into the hills, and the earth has been stained red ever since.

Good News

While these people actually lived, the events of this story aren't true. Seremonda and Raimon didn't have a happy marriage, but they apparently divorced and Seremonda remarried in 1210, then at some later date, she married for the third time. Raimon was still alive around 1218, and historians feel certain that Guillem outlived him. So, don't worry – no one ate anyone's heart.

I hope it wasn't my cooking!

There's Ochre in Them There Hills

Of course, today we don't attribute red soil to either fire or blood, but to iron oxide: it's much less tragic and easier to believe. These natural pigments in the earth are called ochre and they range in color from yellow, orange, red, and brown to deep violet. They have been used in decoration since prehistory and can still be seen in some cave paintings in the area.

Centuries ago, the Romans mined ochre in Provence. But when their empire fell, the knowledge of how to separate the ochre from the soil disappeared along with it. The ochre lay undisturbed until the end of the eighteenth century, when the method was rediscovered and miners began tunneling through the red hills.

From 1910 to 1930 the mines in the area were at their peak. Ochre was used in many products, including makeup and even chocolate. However, when chemical colorants came on the market in the 1920s and 1930s, the ochre mines went into decline.

The village of Roussillon had to adapt, and it replaced mining with tourism. It has now become a enclave of artists who love to use the natural ochre pigments which are readily available in the area. It seems the other residents like to use it too, since most of the buildings in Roussillon are painted in colors that blend seamlessly with the earth, washing the town in an ochre-colored harmony.

Ochre Related Things to Do

Ochre Walks: The Ochre Trail (*Sentier des Ocres*) in Roussillon offers a choice of two trails: one is 30 minutes long, and the other one takes about an hour.

Former Ochre Factory: The *Conservatoire des Ocres et de la Couleur* is just outside Roussillon. Here you can take a tour of the former factory and participate in art workshops.

Hiking: The Provençal Colorado near Rustrel is the site of a former ochre mine. The area is a bit rugged and wild, and you can either hike on your own or take a guided tour.

*Always check with the local tourist office for opening times and availability.

Prints of Provence

Les Indiennes

How did a fabric that originated in India, was copied by Armenians, and outlawed in France become a symbol of Provence?

The kaleidoscope of cotton fabrics that punctuate the Provençal markets today just seem to shout "southern France." They are decorated with cicadas, olives, and flowers in colors that reflect the local landscape: sky blue, sunflower yellow, lavender purple, olive green, and reds reminiscent of the hills of Roussillon. What could be more Provençal? ...Or Indian?

These vibrantly-colored textiles are called *les indiennes* ("Indians"). Their story begins in the mid-seventeenth century, when Armenian merchants, who were living in Marseille to take advantage of the port's tax-free status, ordered them from India.

The Armenians thought the French might take a fancy to this colorful, lightweight, and easy-care cotton cloth, and they were right. It was an instant success among the nobility, and in no time at all it was the fabric to be seen in at the couture-conscious court of Louis XIV.

King Louis was quite the stylish king, prancing around his châteaux in layers of ruffles and lace, exposing his silk stockings and red-heeled shoes. He prided himself on being able to spot a fashion trend, and he knew this one was going to be big. He wanted to get in on it and make some money for his country at the same time. So he directed his Minister of Finance, Jean Baptiste Colbert, who had formed the French East India Company, to start importing these exotic cotton fabrics which soon adorned every noble in the kingdom.

Meanwhile, back in Marseille, when the Armenians saw how popular their cotton cloth was, they had an idea: in addition to selling the expensive Indian fabric to the rich, they would make their own cheaper version of it for the less rich. The common person could watch their budget and still don brightly-colored textiles and feel like an aristocrat.

The nobles loved their expensive Indian fabrics, and the peasants were just as pleased with their knockoffs. Everyone was happy. That is, everyone except the other textile producers. The linen, wool, and silk industries which Louis XIV and Colbert had established in France were feeling the effects of the new cotton competition, and they didn't like it. They all got together and convinced the King that he had to do something. So, in an effort to save the other manufacturers, King Louis went against his fashion sense and banned the brightly-colored cottons that had become a favorite at his court. In 1696, he made it illegal to produce, trade in, or even to wear those popular prints – both imports and knockoffs.

Seventeen years later, the King loosened the ban slightly when he made an exception for the city of Marseille. The fabrics could be produced only in Marseille, and the cloth could only be sold to the colonies and foreign countries. It was still illegal to trade in or wear them in the rest of France.

Finally, in 1759, after 73 years of banishment, these colorful cottons were allowed back into France. King Louis XV realized that the fabrics were no longer the threat to his country that they had been during his grandfather's reign.

Now that the cotton fabric trade was once again legal in all of France, manufacturers started popping up all over Provence, and soon France was again blanketed by the popular prints. New designs were created, and the Indian swirls were eventually replaced by locally-inspired images: cicadas, olives, sunflowers, and lavender in the colors of the Provence landscape.

This once exotic fabric is as popular today as ever and has found new uses. In the Provençal markets you will find a seemingly endless array of tablecloths, kitchen towels, placemats, curtains, etc. Basically, anything made of cloth can be found in these colorful *indienne* prints which brighten up a home with the spirit of Provence.

Even though this fabric came from far-off India, the people of Provence welcomed it with open arms, adopted it, adapted it, and made it their own.

- The great French playwright, Molière, made an allusion to the bourgeoisie, who took to wearing this fabric to imitate the nobles. In *Le Bourgeois Gentilhomme* (1670), Monsieur Jourdain, who tries so hard to be aristocratic but never quite manages it, has a dressing gown made for himself out of this fashionable fabric. But unfortunately, the poor man gets the print upside down and just ends up looking ridiculous.

Did you see the marquise's new dress?
I have an apron in the very same fabric.

PART 2:
IN THE FOOTSTEPS
OF SAINTS

Saints in Boats

Most cultures have been colored by religion and in the case of France, that colorful religion was Christianity.

Around 43 AD Christianity entered Provence when a few boatloads of early Christians washed up on its shores. They had been expelled from the Holy Land and put out into the Mediterranean Sea in small boats without oars or sails. It was meant to be a death sentence, but miraculously their unsteerable vessels carried them straight to the Promised Land of Provence.

These saints in boats made quite an impact, and a few hundred years later, the entire country was Christianized. This religion, along with its saints and miracles, is interwoven with Provençal history and legend.

Martha and the Dragon

One of the boatloads of saints that washed up near Marseille is said to have carried three siblings who had been friends with Jesus: they were Lazarus, Mary Magdalene, and Martha.

Lazarus, who had been miraculously raised from the dead, settled in Marseille where he became the first bishop and then a martyr in his old age. Mary Magdalene, the former loose woman, made her way to Sainte Baume where she dwelt in a cave and spent the rest of her days in prayer. Martha went to preach in the area around Avignon where she made her fame by taming a fierce dragon. This is her story...

St. Martha and the Tarasque

In those days, there was a fearsome monster terrorizing the banks of the Rhone River between Avignon and Arles. This horrendous creature was called a Tarasque. He was the size of a bull, with the face of a lion and razor-sharp teeth. His body was similar to a dragon's, and he had six legs ending in claws so sharp that one swipe could slice a boat in half. On his back was an armored shell like that of a turtle but covered with spikes, and he had a deadly tail that he used like a whip.

This monster killed every living creature that crossed his path: man or beast, on land or in the river. He could shoot fire from his eyes and his mouth, and even his breath would burn whatever it touched. Legions of soldiers went out to fight him, but their spears and weapons were useless against his impenetrable shell.

One day, Martha wandered up that way and started to preach about miracles. After all, she had seen Jesus raise her brother, Lazarus, from the dead. The crowd was a little skeptical and someone suggested that if she could perform a miracle for them they would surely all convert. They proposed that she get rid of the Tarasque, that troublesome dragon that had been eating their kinfolk.

Although Martha had been hoping for an easier task, she took up the challenge. Trembling a bit, she headed for the forest to face the fearsome creature. Everyone applauded her courage then they waved goodbye and never expected to see the poor woman again.

The brave Martha came upon the dragon in the middle of his dinner. He was gobbling up a hapless fellow who had wandered too close to his lair. She plucked up her courage and threw some holy water on the Tarasque. His fiery breath was immediately extinguished. Then she held up a cross, and that was all it took, the monster was instantly subdued. He meekly lumbered up to the saint like a little lamb. She slipped her belt around his neck and gently led him back toward the village.

When the townspeople saw Martha leading the dragon toward them, they couldn't believe their eyes. They were filled with fear and hatred and immediately started to throw stones and spears at the monster. But their assaults just bounced off his back and the now docile beast offered no retaliation.

The people had so much hostility toward the Tarasque who had killed their neighbors and livestock that they just kept throwing things and shouting at him, cursing him for all the pain he had caused. The poor creature, whose character had been completely changed by his conversion, lay down and died of shame for his past actions.

Martha had resolved the monster situation, and no one could deny that it was a miracle. So, most of the town heeded Martha's words and converted to Christianity. In honor of this miracle, the town, which up until this time had been known as Nerluc, changed its name to Tarascon after the Tarasque. And the dragon that everyone was so keen to be rid of is now found on the city's coat of arms. There is a stone statue in his honor near King René's castle, and there is even a special festival every year in remembrance of this story...

Tarasque Festival

The Tarasque festival was started in 1469 by King René of Anjou. At the beginning, it was celebrated on the second Sunday after Pentecost and was seen as a way to ward off evil and floods, for which the Tarasque had previously been blamed.

Of course, nowadays, we understand that dragons don't cause floods, but that's no reason to give up a fun parade. The festivities now take place on the last weekend in June with a large effigy of the Tarasque paraded through the streets as the star of the show.

The Tarasque has even gained worldwide fame: The story of Saint Martha and the Tarasque has been recognized by UNESCO and placed on the list of Masterpieces of the Oral and Intangible Heritage of Humanity. The scientific community also paid homage to the Provençal dragon in 1991 when a newly discovered genus of dinosaur was named Tarascosaurus after the Tarasque. And finally, the fantasy role-playing game, *Dungeons and Dragons*, also features a Tarasque.

Other Dragons

The Tarasque wasn't the only dragon in the area. In the town of Draguignan in the Var region, we find the Tarasque's cousin. He was called the Drac and the town was named for him. As it turns out, he was also vanquished by a saint: Saint Hermentaire, a fifth-century priest from Antibes, slew the monster and freed the inhabitants of the town. In the sixteenth century, Jean de Nostredame (brother to the famous Nostradamus) wrote about this battle between the Saint and the Drac.

It seems that in days gone by, the climate of Provence was quite agreeable to dragons. While the Tarasque and the Drac are the better-known Provençal monsters, many other towns have their own dragon stories: Could it be that Provence was once full of dragons before the saints arrived to vanquish them? On ancient maps was it marked, "Here be Dragons"?

- An interesting note: There is a British folk tale that continues the story of Martha and the dragon. It says that after the beast died and its body was thrown outside the city, Martha went out and resurrected it and it became her pet. She would take it with her on her travels like a little dog. It's said she went to Surrey, England where she and her pet dragon both died. Just outside Guildford, there is a hill with St. Martha's Church on top. Supposedly, the hill is where the dragon is buried.

Saints and Gypsies

A bit west of Marseille, where Martha the dragon-slayer and her siblings landed, another little oarless skiff washed up on shore. It carried two more exiled Christians – two ladies who both happened to be called Mary.

The place they landed is now the town of Saintes-Maries-de-la-Mer which means Saint Marys of the Sea. It's named after these two ladies who went on to become saints. They were Mary Jacobe, sister of the Virgin Mary, and Mary Salome, mother of the apostles, John and James.

Mary J. and Mary S. were your typical saints, going around doing good deeds, converting people, etc. But there's another, more unusual saint in this story: a mysterious, dark-skinned woman called Sara. The church claims she was the Egyptian servant of Mary S. back in Palestine, who jumped into the boat with her mistress at the last minute as it was pushed out to sea.

But according to Gypsy legend, Sara was a local Gypsy queen, already living in Provence before the two Marys arrived. One day, she had a vision of two holy women arriving in a boat and, sure enough, a few days later, she looked out to sea and there was a boat with two women in it drifting toward the shore. Sara took off her cloak, threw it into the water, and used it as a raft to go out and meet them.

Sara welcomed the voyage-weary Marys, giving them food and drink, and she soon became their first convert to Christianity. She stayed and worked with them for the rest of her life. It's said that the job of *Sara la Kâli* (Black Sara), as the Gypsies call her, was to travel around collecting alms for the poor. This might be one reason she is associated with the Gypsies who are often seen on the streets asking for money.

Bones of Saints

The two Marys and Sara did their jobs well, and many people converted to Christianity. When Mary J. and Mary S. died, they were buried near each other and a church was built over their graves. Sara's burial site is unknown.

At some point along the way, both Marys were granted sainthood, and in 1448, King René of Anjou authorized a little archaeological exploration to look for their remains. At this time in history every church altar contained relics of saints and the more saints' relics a church had, the more important it was as a pilgrimage site. So, the floor of the church in Saintes-Maries-de-la-Mer was excavated, and about six feet down, two skeletons were discovered which were said to be "giving off a sweet scent." They were declared to be the bones of the two Marys. They were washed in white wine and placed in a double shrine which was then installed in an upper chapel of the church where it can still be seen today.

In addition to this shrine, the church displays a carved wooden statue of two women in a boat which symbolizes the arrival of the two saints. This carving plays an important part in pilgrimage ceremonies when it is carried to the sea for a blessing.

And where is Sara in all this? Don't worry, she hasn't been forgotten. Although Sara's burial place is unknown and the church has never officially granted her sainthood, she is still known as Saint Sara of the Gypsies. And Gypsies from all parts of Europe make the pilgrimage to this small town each year to venerate her statue located in the church crypt. The statue of this black woman is bedecked with jewelry and dressed in layers of robes which are brought every year by Gypsies to adorn their saint.

The two Marys might be "official" saints, but my followers have more fun... Plus, they bring me jewelry and pretty clothes!

St. Sara of the Gypsies

Gypsy Pilgrimage

Sara's true identity remains a mystery and how she became associated with the Gypsies is unknown as well. She seems to have been venerated in the church in Saintes-Maries-de-la-Mer since the Middle Ages, but the Gypsies only started coming around 1850 – and that's when things started to liven up.

Every May, thousands of Gypsies from all over Europe roll into the small seaside town to celebrate with the residents and other pilgrims. The little town of 2,500 inhabitants plays host to more than 20,000 guests – the majority of them Gypsies. Their influence turns the gathering into a strange blend of religious ceremony, party, and tourist attraction.

The festivities begin on May 24. After a church service, the statue of Sara is brought up from the crypt and carried to the sea by the Gypsies. They are accompanied by men on horseback and other pilgrims, and the entire procession walks right into the water where the statue is blessed in a short ceremony.

The next day, the 25th, is the feast day of Saint Mary Jacobe. After mass, the statue of the two Marys in their boat is carried out to sea. After another watery blessing, everyone heads back to the church.

No one wants to stop the festivities, so the day after the religious services is a day to celebrate the Marquis de Baroncelli, the man who worked to establish these traditions. That evening, there is entertainment in the arena which includes traditional dances and bull games.

- Mary Salome isn't forgotten either. Her feast day is in October, and there is another procession for her. But in October, Sara and the Gypsies don't participate, and it's much quieter without their presence.

From Whence did Gypsies Come?

Gypsies, also known as Roma, Romani, and Travelers in English and *Roms*, *Roma*, *Gitans*, and *Tziganes* in French are a mysterious people. Their origin is almost as puzzling as that of their Saint Sara. These bands of travelers arrived in Europe around the fourteenth century and were called Gypsies (a form of "Egyptian") because they were thought to have come from Egypt. For many years, the birthplace of these nomadic tribes was unknown, but now linguistic and DNA evidence shows that they came from northern India.

They left India as a group and traveled westward, eventually showing up in Europe where a large percentage of them still live. Today, however, there are Gypsies living in almost every country in the world.

Wherever they live, the Gypsies keep their own language and traditions alive, and they tend to keep their distance from other cultures. Possibly because of this separateness, they have been persecuted throughout history. In many regions, they were expelled, enslaved, or even put to death.

Being a mysterious people, they have captured the imagination of many and are represented in literature, film, and art. Sometimes they're portrayed as criminals and at other times their lifestyle is romanticized. One of the most well-known romanticized Gypsies in literature is Esmeralda in Victor Hugo's novel *The Hunchback of Notre-Dame* (or *Notre Dame de Paris* in French). Esmeralda, like most Gypsies, is associated with music, dancing, and fortune-telling.

A Persian Legend

An old Persian legend seeks to explain the origin of Gypsies. In the mid 400s, the Persian king, Bahram V Gor, was shocked to hear that the poor among his subjects didn't have the opportunity to enjoy good music. To rectify this situation, he asked the King of India to send him 10,000 musicians: men and women skilled at playing stringed instruments.

When the musicians arrived, King Bahram gave each one of them an ox, a donkey, a wagon, and a supply of wheat. They were instructed to settle among the farmers, plant their wheat with the help of their ox, and play their beautiful music to sweeten the lives of their neighbors.

But instead of following instructions, the Indian sitar-players ground their wheat for bread and made oxen sandwiches to eat as they traveled around in their donkey-powered wagons, singing, dancing, and generally having a good time. After a year, they were destitute and went back to beg the King for more. King Bahram wasn't amused. He banished them from his kingdom, and the King of

India banned them from India as well because they had embarrassed him. They were doomed to wander the world in their wagons forever, playing their music and trying to earn a little money.

Another myth says that when India was going through a social restructuring and the caste system was put into place, some groups, such as musicians, were left out completely. These people banded together and left India, becoming the wandering Gypsies we know today.

Although we can't be sure how the Gypsies came to Europe, we know where many of them head each year in May. Their participation in the annual pilgrimage to Saintes-Maries-de-la-Mer certainly enlivens the town and adds an extra flavor to the May festivities.

- There is another version of the "Marys in the boat." Some say that the siblings from the previous story (Lazarus, Mary Magdalene, and Martha) were also in this boat and they all landed in Saintes-Maries-de-la-Mer together before heading their separate ways.

Ben and the Bridge

The Avignon Bridge

One thousand years after the first boatload of cast-out Christians landed in Provence, saints were still roaming the land and performing miracles. The famous bridge in Avignon is considered one of those miracles.

Anyone who has ever studied French will have heard of the famous children's song, *Sur le Pont d'Avignon*, about dancing on the Avignon bridge. But if you visit Avignon today, you might be a bit disappointed to see the short section that remains. It's just a fraction of the bridge that once was.

In its day, the Pont d'Avignon was a sight to behold. It was 915 meters (3,000 feet) long and a narrow 2.5 meters (8 feet) wide. Twenty-two arches carried it across the wide Rhone River and the island in the middle. Instead of crossing the river in a straight line, it meandered in (more or less) the shape of a wide "V." This shape helped to break the force of the current. It was the only bridge crossing the Rhone River for more than 200 miles – from Lyon down to the

Mediterranean Sea – and in the Middle Ages, it certainly seemed like a miraculous bit of construction.

The bridge known around the world as the Pont d'Avignon is actually Pont St. Bénezet. It's named after the young man who attained sainthood because of his efforts in building it. This is his story...

Ben and the Bridge

One sunny Sunday in 1177, the people of Avignon were gathered in their church listening to the priest talk about the miracles of God when a boy, probably about 12 years old, burst through the big wooden doors. He was nearly out of breath as he made his way to the front of the church.

"My name is Bénezet, and I come from Vivarais in the mountains of the Ardèche," he announced. "And God spoke to me and told me to come here and build a bridge across the Rhone River."

The congregation raised their eyebrows and looked at scrawny young Bénezet. He looked more like a shepherd than a construction worker. They couldn't help but laugh and whisper among themselves that he must be *fada* (possessed by fairies or a bit crazy).

The priest was of the same opinion and he whispered to a man near him to go get the sheriff. Meanwhile, he tried to reason with the boy and keep him calm.

The priest smiled and said, "My son, can I call you Ben? OK Ben, I'm sure you have the best of intentions, but have you ever built a bridge before? Do you have the money to build a bridge? What makes you think you will be able to do it?"

Ben turned to face the congregation and began to recount his story enthusiastically and with the utmost sincerity.

"I can only tell you what happened. I was out in the fields tending my mother's sheep when I heard a voice speak to me from the heavens. It said, 'Bénezet, listen to me.'

"Of course, I was shocked and asked, 'Who are you?'

"The voice said, 'I am God, and I have a job for you to do. I want you to go to Avignon and build a bridge across the mighty Rhone River.'

"I looked up to the sky and said, 'How can I build a bridge? I'm just a shepherd, and I've never built anything.' I reached into my pocket and pulled out three copper coins. I held them up to the heavens, 'Is this enough to build a bridge over the Rhone?'

"The voice said, 'You just leave everything to me. I'll teach you what you need to know, and I'll provide the necessary funds.'

"So, of course, I followed the voice down from the mountain, and it led me right here to you. And here I am, at your service, ready to build the bridge that God has told me to build."

The people had been held spellbound by Ben's tale and amused by his confidence, but when he finished his story, once again they started to laugh at this slip of a boy who wanted to build a bridge across the treacherous Rhone River.

In the meantime, the sheriff had arrived and heard enough of Ben's story to be intrigued. He walked up to the front of the church and took Ben by the arm. He said, "Well, Boy, if it's really God who told you to do this, then I'm sure you won't mind proving it. We will be most happy to watch you lay the foundation stone for this bridge of yours. And we just happen to have the perfect stone out in the courtyard."

Ben enthusiastically agreed that this was a wonderful idea and confidently followed the sheriff outside. The priest and the congregation were right behind them. In the courtyard of the church was a huge boulder that not even 30 men could budge. Smiling, the sheriff said, "Don't you think this will be the perfect foundation stone? Why don't you carry it down to the water's edge?"

Ben was all smiles as he looked at the stone which outweighed him many times over. He bent down to reach as far as he could around the huge rock. Then he stood up, lifting the stone like it was a feather. He carried it to the water's edge and hurled it into the river. Everyone stood open-mouthed before what surely had to be a miracle.

People started to reach into their pockets and give Ben money for his bridge project. That day, he raised 5,000 sous and started to buy the supplies needed for the construction.

It's perfect ! Now, I'll just carry it down to the river...

As it turned out, Ben wasn't really an engineer and he had no idea how to build a bridge. His talent lay in telling his moving story and raising funds. He founded the Brotherhood of the Bridge, a group of monks that went around spreading the news of Ben's miracle and collecting money for the construction of the bridge, the great Pont d'Avignon.

- Benezet was born in 1163 and died in 1184, one year before the bridge was finished. He was only about 20 years old. He was buried on the bridge itself in the Saint Nicolas Chapel, which is still standing today above the second arch. In 1669, however, a flood washed away part of the bridge and Ben's casket along with it. Fortunately, his bones were recovered and moved to the Celestine Cloister, then later to the church of Saint Didier in Avignon. Ben was later declared a saint, and the bridge is named after him – Pont Saint Bénezet.

- Ben founded the Brotherhood of the Bridge which raised funds for the Avignon Bridge. Legend has it that this organization spread throughout France and funded many other bridge-building projects. However, this has been called into doubt by many historians.

- Construction started on this bridge in 1177 and finished in 1185. But the Rhone is a strong, fast-moving river given to flooding, so parts of this great bridge were always collapsing and being rebuilt. Finally, in the seventeenth century, after 500 or so years of patching it up, the repairmen just threw up their hands, and the bridge was gradually swallowed by the river – except for the small section you can visit today.

Guillaume and Flamenca: A Love Story

Around the same time that Ben was building the great bridge in Avignon, another story was taking place: The Count of Nemours was arranging a marriage for his daughter, Flamenca. Flamenca was beautiful, kind, and full of life, and her husband-to-be, Archambaud, was pleased to have arranged such a marriage for himself.

Flamenca didn't love Archambaud, but she had no say in the matter. She was married off to Archambaud who was very controlling, and Flamenca resigned herself to living unhappily ever after.

Then one day, the young, rich, and handsome Monsieur Guillaume de Nevers rode into town. He looked up into a window and saw Flamenca brushing her long, dark hair. She looked so sad and so beautiful that he immediately fell in love and wanted to rescue her – as so often happens in fairy tales. He asked around and discovered the sad news: the woman of his dreams was married to a man she didn't love, who only let her leave the house to go to church and, even then, made sure she was always supervised.

The next Sunday, Guillaume went to church – as did everyone else in town. The preacher gave a wonderful sermon about treating everyone with love and fairness. Archambaud was there and his head hung low as he felt the weight of guilt about the way he treated his wife. On the other side of the church, Guillaume was feeling inspired.

After the service, Guillaume pulled the priest off to the side. "Father, I think I have an idea that will make everyone happy – even you." The priest nodded for him to continue. "You know that I'm a very rich man. But I'm ready to give up half of all my worldly possessions – which is quite a tidy sum." The priest was all ears, so Guillaume went on to tell him about his love for Flamenca and how her husband was cruel to her and how he (Guillaume) wanted to marry her. He needed to get Archambaud out of the way, but didn't want any harm to come to him.

If the priest could help him, Guillaume would give one quarter of his wealth to Bénezet to finish the Avignon bridge and another quarter to the priest to use for whatever good works he saw fit.

Guillaume had the priest's full attention now, so he continued, "If Archambaud were to leave his wife to take up the religious life, it seems that everyone would be happy. Archambaud could cleanse his soul from the pain he has caused his wife, Flamenca would be free from her loveless marriage, I would be free to woo Flamenca, the Avignon bridge could be finished, and you could do many good works with all the money that would come to you."

The priest was enthusiastic about this idea (and his reward) and he upheld his end of the bargain. He convinced Archambaud that his true calling was that of a monk and in order to fulfill it, he had to leave his wife. When Archambaud broke the "bad news" to Flamenca, he was disappointed that she showed not even the slightest sign of regret.

Archambaud went off to the monastery, and the day he took his vows, a wagon pulled up in front of Bénezet the bridge-builder's home. It was full of enough gold to buy all the remaining materials needed to finish the Avignon bridge. And another wagon full of gold was unloaded at the priest's house.

Bénezet and the Brothers of the Bridge went to work, and the great Avignon Bridge was finished. To celebrate, there was a grand procession across the bridge. The Brothers of the Bridge led the way, followed by all the workers, then the townspeople took to the bridge. They were accompanied by music and dancing, and everyone was so filled with joy that no one even noticed the handsome young man and the beautiful young woman who were leading the dance: Guillaume and Flamenca. The two lovers were the first to dance across the bridge, and it has been a place for lovers ever since.

Sur le Pont d'Avignon
Singing About the Bridge

The Avignon bridge is known around the world today because of the famous children's song, *Sur le Pont d'Avignon* (On the Bridge of Avignon).

People started singing about this miraculous landmark as far back as the fifteenth century, when it was referred to in "pillow songs," songs sung to newlyweds at midnight as they were served soup in their bedroom. It's a mystery to me why people would go into the newlyweds' bedroom and sing about a bridge (or anything else for that matter) but I guess those were different times.

The children's song is about dancing *sur* (on) the bridge of Avignon, but did people ever really dance on the bridge, or did they actually sing on the bridge and dance under it?

One of the first known printed versions of a song using the phrase "*sur le pont d'Avignon*" comes from Venice in 1503. But this song talks about one's beloved *walking* across the bridge – not dancing on it.

Then in 1575 another manuscript uses the phrase "*sur le pont d'Avignon*" but it talks about *singing* on the bridge. The phrase shows up in other songs from 1602, 1613, and 1711, and in all of them, people are still singing on the bridge – no dancing to be found.

So, it seems that up until the late 1600s, when the bridge was washed away, people only walked across, and sang upon, the Avignon bridge. It's highly unlikely that it was ever a place for dancing.

The "dancing on the bridge" form of the song that we know today, seems to have been sung after the original bridge had been washed away and is probably more a romantic idea than actual fact.

The Pont d'Avignon was not a wide bridge. At only 2.5 meters (8 feet) wide, there wouldn't have been enough room to dance around in a big circle like the chorus of this song suggests: they all danced "*tous en rond.*" In addition, the bridge would have been a dangerous place to dance. It was known for being very slippery, and accidents involving horses, wagons, and people slipping off the bridge into the water were not uncommon. Add the strong Mistral wind that blows right down the Rhone River into the mix, and we can imagine that even if people had started out dancing *sur* (on) the bridge, they probably would have ended up *sous* (under) it.

Dancing under the bridge would have been a much safer choice. You might wonder how people could have done that, since normally dancing under a bridge means dancing in the water – but not in this case. The remnants of the bridge that we see today in Avignon barely reach out into the Rhone River, with only four of the original 22 arches remaining. In the Middle Ages, however, the bridge spanned the entire river and crossed a large island in the middle. On this island, under the bridge, there were restaurants and places of entertainment where dances were held. It was probably there that people danced *sous* (under) *le pont d'Avignon* and not *sur* (on) it.

The current version of the song, which talks about dancing *on* the bridge, seems to have come from an eighteenth-century operetta set in Avignon and called *Le Sourd ou l'Auberge Pleine* ("The Deaf Man or the Full Inn"). This musical was reworked several times throughout the years and spread the song's fame worldwide. Then in 1843 the song was published, in a form very close to the one we know today in a book of songs and dances for children.

So, it looks like people only walked across the *Pont d'Avignon* during the Middle Ages and occasionally sang on it. But they probably never danced on it for fear of slipping and falling into the water or being blown off by the Mistral wind.

The original bridge was long gone by the time people started to sing about dancing on it... but still, it does make a lovely song and dance for children.

Sur le Pont d'Avignon
Modern Version

Chorus

Sur le pont d'Avignon,
On y danse, on y danse,
Sur le pont d'Avignon,
On y danse, tous en rond.

On the bridge of Avignon
There we dance, there we dance
On the bridge of Avignon
There we dance, all in a circle.

Verse 1

Les beaux messieurs font comme ça,
Et puis encore comme ça.

The handsome gentlemen go like this, (accompanied by a bow or other action)
And then again, like this.

Chorus

Verse 2

Les belles dames font comme ça,
Et puis encore comme ça.

The beautiful ladies go like this, (accompanied by a curtsy or other action)
And then again, like this.

Chorus

Verse 3...
Different occupations (cobblers, laundresses, gardeners, seamstresses...) or groups of people (young boys, young girls...) all have their verses to dance to. It's a never-ending song as you can always add another occupation or another group of people to "*fait comme ça*" and keep the song going.

Popes in Avignon

Did you know that during the fourteenth century the headquarters for the Catholic Church was in Avignon instead of Rome? Over a span of 67 years (1309–1377) seven popes managed their affairs from this Provençal city and after that, there were even a few antipopes who resided there. But our story begins a bit earlier, when one Italian pope in Rome tried to take on the King of France.

Italian Popes and the French King

In the early 1300s, Pope Boniface VIII, who was Italian and ruling from Rome, had a run-in with King Philippe of France. Philippe declared that all churches in his country would have to pay taxes. And that wasn't all: he had the crazy idea that the clergy should be judged by the State if they broke any laws. Up until that time, religious leaders had been accountable only to church officials, who were much more lenient in their definition of criminal activity and in their methods of punishment.

Boniface was incensed. How dare a mere king go against him! So, he proclaimed that the Church was superior to all kings and all governments, and that church leaders were in no way subject to the laws of men. He forbade any members of his clergy to pay taxes, then he threatened to excommunicate any king who would be so foolhardy as to try and tax them without his consent.

King Philippe apparently wasn't a very good Catholic, because he wasn't at all bothered by the menace of excommunication. He defiantly burned the Pope's declaration and stopped the clergy from sending any gold or silver out of the country. In addition, he stopped all French financial support to the papacy. Then King Philippe went even further and had a bishop arrested on charges of treason.

This really got Boniface all riled up and he declared that he would dethrone Philip and ban all of France from Catholic church services. Philippe stood his ground and the French Parliament backed him up, proclaiming that the king was answerable only to God.

But Boniface just couldn't let it go, and he continued making threats against the King and France. When Philippe had finally had enough, he sent a posse to Rome to arrest the Pope. They roughed him up and threw him into prison just outside of Rome where they left him to think about his actions. But the people still respected the pope's office, and they were outraged. Boniface was released but died within a month from the injuries he received in prison.

The next elected pope was Benedict XI, another Italian pope who died after only nine months from a suspected poisoning. After his death, there was about a year where the church was popeless because the French and Italian cardinals, who were pretty much equally divided, couldn't come to an agreement.

French Popes Like France

Finally, the cardinals settled on Clement V as the new pope – a French pope. The newly elected Frenchman was in Bordeaux – probably munching on a baguette – when he got word of his promotion and was summoned to Rome for his coronation. After calmly finishing his baguette, Clement announced that he would have his ceremony in Lyon, France instead of Rome.

The new pope's friend, King Philippe, attended the ceremony, and Clement immediately appointed nine more French cardinals putting the French firmly in the majority. After his coronation, Clement set up his Papal Court in Poitiers, France. He had no desire to go to Rome. The city was a mess: the previous popes had been in the habit of collecting taxes and using the money for their own purposes instead of reinvesting it in the city which was falling into ruin. The Romans were fed up. They had stopped paying their taxes and were rioting in the streets. No, Clement would rather stay in *la douce France* (sweet France).

In 1309, after four years of holding court in Poitiers, Clement moved the Papal Court to Avignon where it would stay for the next 67 years. At that time, the Papacy owned many areas throughout Europe known as Papal States. Avignon was one such property.

With Pope Clement in Avignon, French cardinals and bishops soon followed and their lavish mansions started popping up all around the city. It seems the French cardinals and bishops weren't much better than the Italian ones had been. They too spent most of the contributions they collected on their own luxuries.

When Pope Clement died, he was followed by six more French popes who all stayed in Avignon. When they weren't eating their Bouillabaisse and drinking their Provençal rosé, they were building, or adding rooms to, a magnificent Pope's Palace. Rome was left to deteriorate.

In 1365, after the Papal Court had been away from Rome for 60 years, Urban V started to think about moving back. He ordered repairs to be made and had the city spruced up for his return. He stayed in Rome for three years, then he got a hankering for some of that mouthwatering French bread and headed back to Avignon. When Urban died, Gregory XI finally returned the papal headquarters to Rome, ending the Avignon period for good. Sort of...

No More French Popes

Gregory XI ruled from Rome and died there, which meant the next papal election had to be held in Rome. By this time, most cardinals were French, so the Frenchies controlled the vote. But the people of Rome had made up their minds that there would not be another French pope. They wanted an Italian – one they could count on to stay home and take care of their city. So, as the cardinals walked to the conclave to cast their votes for the new pope, the Romans met them in the streets. They made it clear that it was in the cardinals' best interest to elect an Italian. They even stacked firewood under the room where the conclave was held – ready for a cardinal roast should another Frenchie be elected. Wisely, the cardinals elected an Italian who became Pope Urban VI.

The Antipopes

Italian Urban VI didn't like the French cardinals and made vicious accusations about their overspending and immorality – which were probably all true. He appointed more Italian cardinals to tip the scale of power back to the Italian side.

The French cardinals were so unpopular at the papal court that they had to get out of town. They met just south of Rome where they decided to hold their own conclave. They claimed that they had been forced to choose between voting for Urban VI or being roasted on the bonfire. Surely, they should get a "do-over." So, the French cardinals held their own election and, of course, they chose another Frenchman. They declared Clement VII their new pontiff, and he and all his French cardinals went happily back to Avignon. Now, however, there were two popes, an Italian one in Rome and a French one in Avignon. This became known as the Papal Schism. Clement VII, the Avignon pope, was followed by Benedict XIII, and both were later declared antipopes by the Council of Constance in 1415.

It seems that the seven French popes who ran away to live the Provençal lifestyle in Avignon made quite an impression on the Catholic Church: They have never since elected another French pope.

Papal Recap

Popes in Rome:
Boniface VIII (1294–1303) Italian – fought with the King of France.
Benedict XI (1303–1304) Italian – lasted only nine months.

The Avignon Popes:
Pope Clement V (1305–1314) French – moved to Avignon in 1309.
Pope John XXII (1316–1334) French – started building the Pope's Palace.
Pope Benedict XII (1334–1342) French – finished building the Pope's Palace.
Pope Clement VI (1342–1352) French.
Pope Innocent VI (1352–1362) French.
Pope Urban V (1362–1370) French – lived in Rome three years then went back to Avignon.
Pope Gregory XI (1370–1378) French – moved papacy back to Rome for good.

The Avignon Antipopes:
Clement VII (1378–1394)
Benedict XIII (1394–1423)

- Avignon remained part of the Papal States until the French Revolution, when it became part of France.
- The Pope's Palace (*Palais des Papes*) in Avignon is the largest gothic palace in the world. Many of the rooms in this UNESCO World Heritage Site can be visited.

PART 3:
A FEW CURIOUS
CHARACTERS

Every place likes to ride on the glory of its famous residents, and Provence is no exception. It's dotted with plaques saying "so and so was born here" or "so and so lived here" and the more notable local success stories are honored with statues. In this section, we'll talk about just a few of Provence's curious characters who have left their mark on the region.

Nostradamus

Nostradamus. You've probably heard of this sixteenth-century prophet whose very name conjures up mystery and mysticism. And you've probably read about his many predictions, which may or may not have come to pass. But did you know that Nostradamus was a Provençal lad?

Michel de Nostredame was born in December 1503 in St. Rémy-de-Provence. His ancestors were Jewish, but in the mid-fifteenth century, his grandfather, Guy de Gassonet, converted to Catholicism. The family surname was changed to Nostradame (Notre Dame or Our Lady) because his confirmation took place on Saint Mary's feast day. The name would later be Latinized to Nostradamus. It's possible that Grandad Guy's conversion was for appearances only, because it's said that young Michel learned Jewish mysticism and astrology at his feet.

Apothecary and Doctor

At around the age of 16, young Michel went off to university in Avignon. Unfortunately, after only one year, plague broke out and the school temporarily closed its doors. Since he couldn't continue his studies, Nostradamus became an apothecary. It seems that mixing up medical potions and dispensing them didn't require a diploma in those days. During his time in the pharmacy, he learned a lot about the healing properties of plants and became interested in all things medical.

Nine years later, in 1529, the plague had settled down, and Nostradamus went back to university. This time he went to the University of Montpellier to study for his doctorate in medicine. But there was a little problem. When it was discovered that he had worked as an apothecary, which was considered manual labor, he was expelled. He must have succeeded in getting back in school, however, because he seems to have become a doctor.

Around 1533, at the age of 30, Doctor Nostradamus settled near Toulouse and married Henriette d'Encausse with whom he had two children. Everything went well for about five years, but then Nostradamus was accused of heresy. He had made some offhand remark to workmen building a mold for a statue of the Virgin Mary. Someone reported him and he was "invited" to appear before the Inquisition tribunal in Toulouse to be judged. But Nostradamus felt his services were needed elsewhere – Italy, Turkey, Greece, anywhere but where the trial was to be held.

Unfortunately, while Nostradamus was off dodging the Inquisition, a contagious illness (possibly the plague) struck his family. His wife and both children died. Maybe this is what inspired his tireless work with towns affected by plague.

When plague struck Marseille in 1544, Nostradamus went there to offer his services. Then a few years later, he was called to Aix to help treat victims of plague there. Wherever the disease broke out, Nostradamus would go.

He had put his apothecary skills to good use and had developed an herbal medicine which he claimed could protect from the plague. It was a "rose pill" made of rosehips which, as we now know, are full of vitamin C. He used other methods, unusual for the day: he prescribed good hygiene, fresh air, and disinfecting.

Astrologer, Writer, and Prophet

Around the age of 44, Nostradamus settled in Salon-en-Provence. There he married for the second time to a young widow, Ann Ponsard, with whom he had several children.

The newly-married Doctor Nostradamus took a new direction and became a writer. Most of his written works were produced in his Salon-en-Provence home where he worked in his library, surrounded by books and stargazing paraphernalia.

At the same time that he became an author, he also took a new name: Michel de Nostradame became Michel Nostradamus. Nostradamus started to publish almanacs which contained weather predictions, agricultural tips, medical advice, recipes for making beauty treatments, and – maybe most importantly – lots of mystical prophecies.

He also published a "cookbook" full of recipes for making face creams and jams as well as medical creams. And just to make sure he was on good terms with the Church, he dedicated many of his writings to the Pope.

In 1555 Nostradamus published the first book dedicated solely to his obscure visions, *Les Propheties* (The Prophecies). Each prophecy was written as a four-line poem,

I predict that every recipe will be a success.

and a group of 100 of these was called a century. Nostradamus' predictions were anything but clear. It seems he intentionally made them difficult to interpret by using vague wording, throwing in bits of other languages, and arranging them in non-chronological order.

The Prophet and the Royals

Even though Nostradamus' predictions were pretty much impossible to decipher, everyone wanted to know the future, and his book of prophecies hit the bestseller list. The notables took note, and famous people started asking for astrological readings. In 1555, he was called to the court of King Henri II and Queen Catherine de Medici. The Queen had heard of his prophecies and wanted to know how they related to her family.

Nostradamus wasn't sure what to expect. Were they fans or did they hate his work? He met the royal couple and presented them with a signed copy of his latest book of prophecies which was wisely inscribed "to the most invincible, most powerful, and most Christian Henri II, King of France, Michel Nostradamus, his very humble and very obedient servant and subject, wishes victory and happiness." He wasn't taking any chances.

The King asked Nostradamus if there was anything in the book that pertained to his reign. Nostradamus dodged the question by saying, "This book is filled with secrets that come from God and nature and are next to impossible to interpret."

The King asked again if there was anything he should know. Nostradamus said, "Well, it's always a good idea to beware of young warriors." These words made no sense to the King, so he thanked Nostradamus for the book and sent him on his way. That night, King Henri read the book cover to cover. He found nothing in there that related to him or anything else, as far as he could tell. He concluded that the astrologer was mad as a hatter and that all of his ramblings were nonsensical. He didn't give the crazy old coot a second thought.

A few years later, in the summer of 1559, King Henri hosted a three-day celebration in honor of the marriages of his daughter and his sister. As usual, there was a jousting match. The King wanted to prove that even at age 40, he was still fit and athletic, so he challenged the Count of Montgomery in a joust.

Now, everyone knew that if they were ever pitted against the King that it was good form to let him win. No doubt, Montgomery had intended to do just that. But, as his horse was running full speed ahead toward King Henri, Montgomery was jostled and lost his balance. His lance flew up and went through the eye slit in Henri's helmet. At first, it seemed that the King would recover. But things went from bad to worse and after ten days of suffering, King Henri died.

Scholars searched Nostradamus' writings and found this in Quatrain 1 35:

The young lion shall overcome the old one
On a field of war in a single combat:
He will put out his eyes in a cage of gold:
Two fleets one, then he dies a cruel death.

- Both men had lions on their shields, and Montgomery was younger than Henri.
- The joust took place on the Champs de Mars in Paris which means field of wars.
- Henri's helmet was supposedly adorned with traces of gold.
- The lance is said to have split causing two wounds: one in the eye and one in the temple.

Everyone, including the Queen, was convinced that Nostradamus had correctly foreseen the King's death. Montgomery believed in the prophesy too and hoped that everyone would see that the accident was written in the stars and he wasn't really responsible. Henri forgave him, but later Catherine had him beheaded – he couldn't avoid his date with destiny.

The King's death put Nostradamus and his prophecies in the spotlight, and book sales went through the roof.

Catherine called Nostradamus to Paris to be her personal astronomer, ignoring the other 30,000 astrologers in the city at the time.

Catherine bestowed another honor on Nostradamus in 1564 when she came to visit him in Salon-de-Provence. The Queen named him the doctor and counselor to the new king (her son, Charles IX).

A few years later, in 1566, Nostradamus was 63 years old and very sick. One night he told his servant that he would not find him alive in the morning. And sure enough, the next morning Nostradamus was dead. One folk tale says that in 1700 the city officials decided to move Nostradamus' body to a new resting place. When they opened his grave, they saw on his chest a medallion engraved with the year 1700 – a prediction that he had made 134 years earlier of the year his tomb would be opened.

Another legend describes a curse associated with Nostradamus' grave. Whoever would hold his skull in their hands would be filled with all his knowledge – then immediately, they would die. It was during the French Revolution that three soldiers supposedly dug up his grave. One of them held up the prophet's skull. The other two said his eyes widened in awe – then, the next second, he was shot through the head.

Of course, there is no historical proof for either of these legends. But the question remains: how did Nostradamus see all the tragic events that he wrote about in his books? Some say that he would stare into a brass bowl filled with water and herbs until he went into a trance and began to see visions. Then he would use a method of looking at the alignment of stars when similar historical events had happened to predict when the same celestial configuration would bring about the event he had seen in his vision.

Do his predictions really come true, or are they just vagaries that could be applied to many situations? Either way, his prophecies are still as popular today as ever. After every major event, Nostradamus believers check to see if they can find something in his writings to suggest that he had predicted it.

A few of the events that Nostradamus supposedly predicted are: the French Revolution; Hitler's rise to power; World Wars I and II; dropping of the atomic bomb; two Kennedy assassinations; the 9/11 Twin Tower bombings in New York, and even the Trump presidency.

Didn't he ever see anything pleasant in that bowl of water?

You won't understand my mysterious prophecies until after they come to pass... Then you can look them up in my book and see that I was correct.

So buy my book today! I predict that one day my book will be sold in the Amazon.

What to See and Do

- In Salon-en-Provence, you can visit the house where Nostradamus wrote most of his prophecies which has been turned into a museum. There are two Nostradamus statues to see as well: one is traditional and the other modern and stylized.
- In St. Rémy the house where Nostradamus was born, on 6 rue Hoche, is not open to the public. There is a simple plaque above the door: *Ici Naquit, le 14 Décembre 1503, Michel de Nostradame, dit Nostradamus, Astrologue.*

Tartarin of Tarascon

The Lovable French Country Bumpkin

The Provençal town of Tarascon is mostly associated with the Tarasque and Saint Martha, who delivered the area from the dragon's clutches. However, Martha isn't the only slayer of ferocious beasts whose name is linked with the town. Tarascon's other unlikely hero is Tartarin, a fictional lion hunter in an 1872 novel by Alfonse Daudet, *Tartarin of Tarascon* (*Aventures Prodigieuses de Tartarin de Tarascan* in French). The story goes something like this...

The men of Tarascon had been keen hunters ever since the time of the Tarasque, when they would spend their weekends using the invincible beast as target practice. After Martha took care of the dragon problem, the zealous local lads turned their attention to all the other critters living in the woods around town.

By the time the nineteenth century rolled around, word had spread throughout the animal kingdom to steer clear of Tarascon, and there wasn't a wild animal to be found for miles around. Even migrating birds would avoid flying over the town.

However, the lack of game didn't stop the Tarasconian menfolk from their weekly "hunt." Every Sunday, they packed up a big lunch and several bottles of wine and went out into the countryside. After their picnic, they would start shooting... at their hunting caps. Each "hunter" would throw his hat high into the air and shoot at it. The one whose cap fell to the ground with the most holes in it was declared the greatest hunter. And every week, Tartarin's headgear looked like Swiss cheese. He was admired and respected as the greatest cap hunter in Tarascon.

He was a complicated character, this Tartarin. On the one hand, he was a starry-eyed Provençal Don Quixote craving exciting adventures, and on the other, he was a comfort-loving, pessimistic Sancho Panza. In Tartarin's case, Sancho was just a little bit more influential than Don Quixote.

Tartarin read books about great adventures and he talked of these exploits so often that everyone (including Tartarin himself) began to believe that they were his own. But in truth, he had never actually left his hometown of Tarascon, nor had he shot at anything more ferocious than his cap.

One day a circus came through town and Tartarin saw a lion for the first time. He began to dream of going to Africa to hunt the mighty beast. He read books about great safaris and his conversations were filled with talk of lions. Everyone was very excited to have one of their own going off to hunt the big cats, but after a while, they noticed that Tartarin wasn't making any preparations, and they began to talk.

I'm the greatest hunter in all of Tarascon... Just throw your hat into the air and I'll show you!

The Adventure Begins

When Tartarin realized his reputation as the greatest hunter in Tarascon was in peril, there was only one thing for him to do. He had to go to Africa and hunt lions. He booked passage on a ship to Algeria where he had many misadventures: he hooked-up with a conman; he lost all his money; he shot a donkey, thinking it was a lion (it was night); and finally he shot a real lion. Unfortunately, the lion he shot was a tame, blind lion whose owners moved it from town to town where it sat up and begged holding a bowl in its teeth. In Tartarin's defense, the lion was coming through a field and he didn't see the owners with it.

Tartarin was swindled out of almost everything in Algeria and was left with only two possessions: the lion skin, which he had sent back to Tarascon, and an old camel with a wonky hump that flopped over to one side. This camel had become very attached to Tartarin and followed him around like a puppy. The great hunter was embarrassed by this, and was always trying to ditch the defective camel.

Tartarin didn't have enough money to get home, so he wandered around Algeria until he ran into an old friend, a ship's captain, who offered him free passage back to France. When the ship set sail, Tartarin thought he had finally escaped the camel but it jumped into the sea and swam after the boat. The captain took pity on the poor creature and pulled it aboard. When they arrived in Marseille, a downcast Tartarin boarded the coach for Tarascon and – wouldn't you know it? – the camel trotted along behind.

The Hero Returns

The mighty hunter felt humiliated and dreaded facing his neighbors. But to his surprise, the people of Tarascon gave him a hero's welcome. They had seen the lion skin and assumed that it was just one of many taken down by the greatest hunter in Tarascon. They congratulated him on his fantastic success and Tartarin started to think that maybe he had been rather magnificent after all.

Then the camel trotted up and popped his head around the corner. The people of Tarascon gasped in fear. For a moment they thought that old monster, the Tarasque had returned – but it was just an exotic animal brought back from their heroic hunter's African escapade.

As Tartarin walked toward his home, surrounded by the admiring crowd, and followed by his faithful camel, he began telling amazingly exaggerated tales of his glorious exploits in Africa...

According to Daudet: "The men of Provence don't lie, they are mistaken... They don't always tell the truth, but they believe they do... Their lies aren't really lies, they are more like mirages." But Daudet didn't want anyone to think he was just picking on Provence, so he also wrote: "In France, everyone is a little bit from Tarascon."

While the people of Provence do have a reputation for embellishing the truth, the Tarasconians thought Daudet had gone too far. They wanted his skin. However, the book put Tarascon on the map and brought it a degree of fame, so the locals learned to laugh about Tartarin and even embrace the lovable bumpkin.

The city now has a small museum dedicated to Tartarin, and every June, he participates in the Tarasque parade right along with the town's mythical dragon.

Things to See in Tarascon

- The Tarasque Festival takes place on the last weekend in June
- Tartarin Museum
- Tarasque sculpture
- King René's castle

Gaspard de Besse

Robin Hood Of Provence

Just like Robin Hood, Gaspard de Besse robbed from the rich (who detested him) and gave to the poor (who adored him). But while Robin Hood's roots are shrouded in mystery, there's no doubt about the identity of our French outlaw.

Gaspard Bouis, later known as Gaspard de Besse, was born February 9, 1757 in Besse-sur-Issole, a village in the Var region of southern France. His father was a small landowner and farmer who died one year after Gaspard was born. He was raised by the local priest who assumed the young boy would follow his footsteps into a religious life and made sure he had a proper education.

However, Gaspard was a charming, handsome smooth-talker who wasn't suited to the priestly way of life. At the age of 17 he left the small town of Besse and went to Toulon for a taste of the city. It's in Toulon that he began his life of crime and it's also there that history and myth become a bit entangled.

Why and how did young Gaspard become a criminal? According to some, he saw a poor mother with four children living in appalling circumstances because her husband had been put into forced labor for salt trafficking. Gaspard couldn't abide this and decided to act. He helped the father and another prisoner escape, and these two men became his lieutenants for the new band of outlaws that he soon formed.

Another story says that army recruiters got Gaspard drunk and convinced him to enlist. After he sobered up and realized what had happened, he hot-footed it out of there and hid in the mountains.

However it came about, wanted posters were pasted up all across the south of France bearing pictures of Gaspard's handsome face. Being the resourceful young man that he was, he made the best of his situation and decided it was the ideal time to start a new enterprise. He set up shop in a cave in Mont Vinaigre (Mount Vinegar) near Fréjus, and hung out his "help wanted" sign. Soon he had a band of about 50 robbers working for him.

To work for Gaspard, they had to abide by strict rules: he insisted that even though they carried muskets (which made people more agreeable to handing over their goods) they weren't allowed to shoot anyone. In addition, only the rich could be robbed and part of the takings would be invested back into the community... that is, given to the poor locals. Those who benefited from Gaspard's generosity were very loyal and happy to tip him off and hide him when the police came snooping around.

With the protection of the locals, Gaspard's business flourished. His favorite "clients" were tax collectors and politicians, but any rich traveler would do. Even though he was a bandit, Gaspard never forgot his manners. When he robbed rich ladies, he would turn on the charm, handing out compliments and kissing hands as he slipped the rings off their fingers. He flirted and the ladies blushed. And maybe they didn't even mind handing over their jewels.

As his popularity grew, so did his bravado. Gaspard started to think he was invincible. He even had the audacity to turn up at local balls, dressed like a dandy, sporting fine fabrics and diamond cufflinks. He would mingle among the rich lords and ladies, charm them with his wit, then relieve them of their money and jewels.

But eventually, Gaspard's luck was bound to run out, and in 1779 he was arrested. He was thrown into prison in Draguignan, but escaped a few months later – possibly with the help of the jailer's daughter. Even though Gaspard wasn't there, his trial went ahead as scheduled and he was found guilty of armed robbery in absentia.

But that didn't worry Gaspard, he was happy to be free and carried on robbing from the rich and giving to the poor for another year or so. He worked solely in the south of France, but because his "clients" were from everywhere, his reputation spread far and wide. In 1780, the order came from Paris to the quartermaster of Provence to do whatever it took to arrest that nuisance, Gaspard de Besse. A massive manhunt was conducted throughout the region, but with no luck.

Then one evening, after Gaspard and his merry band had relieved some travelers of their heavy burden in the gorges of Ollioules, they went out to dinner to celebrate. It was in an auberge in La Valette where Gaspard was arrested. One story says that he was captured by accident when someone tipped off the police that there was a band of criminals in the tavern. The lawmen swooped in and arrested them without even knowing it was the infamous Gaspard de Besse and his gang. Another version says he was turned in by a jilted lover.

This time, there was no escape for Gaspard. On October 25, 1781, at 24 years old, Gaspard de Besse was tied to the wheel of torture and met a slow and agonizing death in Aix-en-Provence. After he died, his head was cut off and nailed to a tree at the edge of the Taillades woods where he had carried out many of his robberies.

To the state, Gaspard was a criminal, but to the people, he was a hero. They felt that he took back what the politicians, tax collectors, and money lenders had unfairly taken from them. He had become a legend, and the people fondly remembered him as a big-hearted bandit, and a defender of the poor.

But what about his treasure? Surely, he must have had a fortune stashed away somewhere. With their beloved Gaspard gone, the locals turned their thoughts to finding the riches he left behind. They were sure that's what he would have wanted.

It was rumored that Gaspard's hoard was hidden somewhere in the region of Cuges les Pins, just east of Marseille, and everyone grabbed their shovels and trotted off to look for it. Some searched under the cover of darkness to avoid having to share, should they be the lucky ones to find it. Every château in the area was searched from top to bottom and every field looked like it was infested with moles, but his treasure was never found... as far as we know. Even today, if you are in the area of Cuges les Pins, you might see some people with their metal detectors, still hoping to find Gaspard's hoard.

Good King René

King René's Fountain in Aix-en-Provence

Aix-en-Provence is known as "the city of 1,000 fountains." However, since the folks of this area have a reputation for exaggeration, we should probably take that with a grain of salt. The real number might be closer to 107... but still, it does have a lot of fountains.

One particular fountain caused quite a stir when it was unveiled in 1923. It was to be topped by a statue of a man who played a major role in the history of Aix in the fifteenth century: he was called Good King René. Let's learn a bit more about this intriguing character, then we'll find out what all the fuss was about...

René of Anjou, also known as Good King René (*Bon Roi René*), was a very important man in his day. He had more titles than you could shake a stick at: he was the Count of Provence, Bar, Piedmont, and Guise; the Duke of Calabria, Lorraine, and Anjou; and the King of Hungary, Sicily, Aragon, Valencia, Majorca, Sardinia, Jerusalem, and possibly a few other places.

This multi-titled man played an important role in fifteenth-century Europe and rubbed shoulders with the movers and shakers of the time, so let's do a bit of name-dropping. René's mother financed Joan of Arc's campaign to save France, and René rode right alongside the Maid of Orléans. Christopher Columbus mentioned René as giving him his first commission as captain. And the Good King is said to have inspired Cosimo de Medici to collect manuscripts from around the world and open the first public library in Renaissance Europe, San Marco in Florence.

As if all that wasn't enough, he was a patron of the arts as well as being a writer and artist himself. His gastronomical contributions to Provence include introducing the Muscat grape to the region, and, according to legend, he was behind the creation of the calisson, a specialty candy of Provence.

His Very Own Fountain

So, when this accomplished King/Count/Duke was finally going to be honored by a fountain bearing his likeness, what caused all the kerfuffle?

In 1923, when the big day arrived, the area in front of the covered statue was filled with Aixois (people of Aix-en-Provence) anxious to see their new fountain (number 1,001?) which would pay homage to an important character in their city's history.

As the tarp was pulled off, people prepared to say "Ahhh" in appreciation... instead, however, they all burst into laughter.

This is what they expected to see:
the frumpy, old King they recognized from the painting in
the church.

And this is what they saw: a firmer, more buff version.

Who is it?

The people speculated that since the statue had been made
in Paris, maybe the sculptor had been working on a
likeness of someone else and lost the commission. Perhaps
instead of wasting a perfectly good block of marble, he
recycled it and called it Good King René. After all, René
had already been dead for more than 300 years, and the

sculptor might have assumed that no one would recognize him anyway.

But, as it turned out, the people of Aix had a very clear idea what their Good King looked like. They saw him every Sunday in church. On the triptych in the cathedral was a portrait of the King and his second wife, Jeanne – and the new King René statue didn't look anything like the King René they knew and loved. But they don't take things too seriously in Aix, so they just had a good laugh and left it at that.

To be fair to the artist, though, he was representing a young René, so of course he would look different to the painting of the older, plumper René on the church triptych. But whoever the man in the fountain really is, he holds a cluster of the Muscat grapes which René introduced to the region, and he has books at his feet representing his intellectual interests.

The Good King René fountain is just one of the 1,000 – I mean 107 – or so lovely fountains you will find in this "city of water."

The Sweet Story of
King René and Queen Jeanne

The calisson is a small, distinctive, almond-shaped candy which first appeared in Aix-en-Provence in the fifteenth century, during the reign of Good King René. The following legend is often associated with its creation...

Jeanne de Laval wasn't pleased when she found out that her father had signed a marriage contract with King René. Yes, he was a powerful man who had a lot of titles, which could be an attractive quality... but she was 21 years old and he was an "old man" of 45 years. He was also a widower: his first wife had died the year before, after bearing him nine children, three of whom were still alive and living at home. And what about all his illegitimate children? What could she expect from a philanderer like that?

Jeanne might have preferred a younger, more handsome man, but it was a time in history when daughters had to marry the man their father chose for them, so Jeanne did. She did everything she was supposed to do, but her heart wasn't in it, and she never smiled. The King bought her fine clothes and exquisite jewels. He brought in jesters to perform and tell her jokes. He did everything he could think of to make his wife happy, but to no avail.

In 1457 the royal couple moved to Aix-en-Provence after spending the first three years of their marriage in Angers. A great celebration was held to welcome the new Queen and to introduce her to the people of Aix. King René wanted to make a good impression on his wife and his subjects, so he instructed his Italian chef to whip up a special surprise to be presented after dinner. The result was a treat made of almonds and candied fruit. As a tribute to the new Queen, the chef formed this delicacy in the shape of her lovely, but ever-so-sad eyes.

At the sumptuous meal in her honor, the melancholy Jeanne picked at her food, not really enjoying it. There was music, there were jesters, and everyone seemed to be having a good time – except the Queen. Dessert came around, and she half-heartedly picked up one of the little eye-shaped treats and nibbled at it. It was such a pleasant surprise, that the Queen smiled for the first time since her marriage. Her grin captured the people's hearts and they felt as if she was giving them all little hugs. "Little hugs" in Provençal is *"di calin soun"* and therefore, the delicacy became known as a calisson.

It seems that the queen wasn't grumpy after all, she just wanted something sweet to eat. Once the King realized this and provided her with daily sweets, they had a very happy marriage.

Queen Jeanne
The queen with the
calisson-shaped eyes

The Calisson

Marcel Pagnol, the Provençal writer, explained the calisson recipe like this: "one third almonds, one third candied fruit, one third sugar, and most importantly, one third know-how and love of a job well done..." Well, it's a good thing Pagnol was a writer and not a mathematician.

A more typical recipe for this little sweet is 40% ground almonds and 60% candied fruit, with melon being the fruit of choice. The locally-grown almonds and fruit are made into a paste, then formed into little wafers and topped with white frosting. The original calisson was melon-flavored, but now you can find them in a variety of fruity flavors.

These little sweets probably originated in Italy around the twelfth century, and even if it wasn't actually invented to make Queen Jeanne smile, it did first appear in Provence during King René's reign.

The Calisson Mass

Take Your Caisson
You Don't Want to Catch the Plague!

In 1629 a terrible plague was devastating Aix-en-Provence. The city leaders took drastic measures and confined everyone to their homes. No one was allowed out in the streets, and no one wanted to leave their home and risk infection from the deadly disease.

During this terrible time, the little sweet that had been invented to make Queen Jeanne smile found a new use. It gained a reputation as a protection against the plague. At its base was a wafer, just like the one used in the holy communion service. The almonds and fruit added a little sweetness to the population's daily ordeal – and they also provided health-giving vitamins and antioxidants. Although people didn't know about vitamins and antioxidants at the time, they took their "one-a-day" calisson in hope of staying healthy.

The calissons apparently worked for some, and the plague started to show signs of letting up. In September 1630, a few people decided to venture out and go to Mass to give thanks to Notre Dame de la Seds, the patron saint of Aix. The plague ended, and it became a tradition to celebrate a special Mass in early September to thank God for delivering the city.

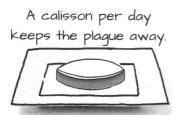

A calisson per day keeps the plague away.

At these special services, instead of the holy wafer being distributed during communion, calissons were distributed. This annual tradition continued until the French Revolution put an end to it –along with most religious services.

The Calisson Mass was revived in 1996, and the date was fixed as the first Sunday in September. It's a day dedicated to Queen Jeanne's sweet treat of Aix. There's a blessing for the calisson makers and a sermon about the importance of sharing the sweetness of life. The rest of the day is filled with traditional music, dance, and of course... callisons for everyone!

If the theory that the calisson's name came from Queen Jeanne's smile feeling like little hugs doesn't sound plausible to you, there is another one with religious origins. Some say the name came from the Latin phrase "venite ad calicem" which is pronounced during the communion service and means "come to the chalice." Translated into Provençal, it is "venes touti au calissoun" which sounds a lot like an invitation for everyone to come and get a calisson.

More Info

- The calisson is one of the 13 desserts served at the traditional Provençal Christmas Eve dinner. While some of these desserts are optional and can be replaced by something else, the calisson is always present. It's non-negotiable! (You can read more about the 13 desserts as well as other traditions in my book, *French Holidays & Traditions*.)
- Calisson Museum – Musée du Calisson, Confiserie du Roy René. You can visit this museum to see how calissons are made, find a bit of history, and buy some tasty treats. Address: 5380 Route d'Avignon (RN7) 13089 Aix-en-Provence www.calisson.com
- The Calisson Mass is the first Sunday in September.
- The statue of King René in Aix-en-Provence is at the end of Cours Mirabeau, an avenue with several other fountains along it.

PART 4:
LANGUAGE AND
CULTURE

In the 1800s, France was a divided nation. There was a huge difference between Paris and the rural areas of France, each of which had their own customs and languages. Many people in these areas didn't even speak French.

France was struggling to transform itself into a homogeneous country with Paris at the center spreading its culture and language to the rest of the nation. Education was centralized and schooling became mandatory, with Paris dictating what the children were taught. And every child, whether Parisian or Provençal, was taught exactly the same things, including the French language, French culture (as defined by Paris), and the idea of nationalism.

Local traditions and languages began to fall by the wayside. But thankfully, some people rushed in to rescue them: people like Frédéric Mistral and the Félibrige...

Freddie and the Félibrige

Frédéric Mistral is to thank, in great part, for reviving the Provençal language and for bringing it worldwide attention when he won the Nobel Prize in Literature in 1904. His writing also recorded, saved, and codified the waning traditions of his beloved Provence.

It's only a coincidence that his last name is the same as the infamous wind that gusts through the region, but just like that wind, Mistral's influence whirls through Provence's language, history, and culture.

It all started one day in 1845, when 15-year-old Freddie was at school. He wasn't paying attention to his French lesson, and he appeared to be daydreaming and scribbling in his notebook. But just when the teacher was about to bust the doodling delinquent, he saw that Freddie was writing a poem – and writing it in his native Provençal language. The teacher was Joseph Roumanille, who was a Provençal poet himself, and he was thrilled to discover young Freddie's talent. Roumanille became Mistral's mentor and encouraged the lad to continue his daydreaming and poetry writing – outside school hours, of course.

After graduating from secondary school, Freddie went to Aix-en-Provence to study law. But he remained a poet at heart and became a crusader for saving the local language and way of life that he loved.

Language of the Troubadours

The Provençal language was too important to lose: it was a form of Occitan, the first literary language of modern Europe. This romance language has a long and rich history: it was the one in which the twelfth-century troubadours wrote and sang their ballads. Through their poetry, the troubadours had spread the ideals of chivalry and courtly love throughout the land.

FRÉDÉRIC MISTRAL

Mistral and Roumanille (his former teacher), joined up with five other kindred spirits, and together the seven Provençal poets saw themselves as a new generation of troubadours. They would use their native language, the same one the medieval troubadours had used, to revive local traditions and awaken a sense of pride in the people of Provence. They would be the courageous knights riding out to rescue their culture and language from being swallowed up by the dragon of modernity. But instead of traveling across the land singing their message, they printed their words in books and sent them out into the world.

The Félibrige

When these new non-musical troubadours held their first meeting in 1854, one item on the agenda was choosing a name. Perhaps they considered calling themselves "Freddie and the Troubadours" (which would have been a great name for a 1960s rock band) but they decided on "The Félibrige." They were inspired by a little Provençal song that told of the time when Jesus was found in the temple debating "with the seven *felibres* (doctors) of the law." They also happened to be a group of seven, and they were setting out to create the new laws of Provençal poetry. So, from the word *felibre*, they invented the word Félibrige and took it as the name of their group.

The seven original members of the Félibrige were: Joseph Roumanille, age 36 (Mistral's former teacher); Frédéric Mistral, age 24; Theodore Aubanel, age 25, whose family owned a printing company (very handy for a group of authors); Anselme Mathieu, age 26, from a winemaking family (also very useful for a group of authors); Jean Brunet, age 32; Paul Giera, age 38; and Alphonse Tavan, age 21. They were all poets and passionate about reviving their native language.

But first things first. In order to promote reading and writing in Provençal, they had to standardize the spelling and grammar of this mainly oral language. They decided to keep the rules simple, so everyone could easily grasp them. (If only they could have done the same with French!)

The Félibrige's first publication, in 1855, was the *Armana Prouvençau*, an almanac written entirely in the Provençal language. It told of upcoming holidays and festivals, and also contained a history of Provence to help people understand and take pride in their past. By writing about Provence and the Provençal way of life in the local language, the Félibrige was preserving both the language and the culture.

Mistral's Works

At the same time as the Félibrige was recording and saving the old ways, they created at least one new symbol. It's thanks to Frédéric Mistral that the cicada is now the mascot of Provence. Freddie decided to use the noisy little insect's image on his bookplate and soon they were being produced in ceramic and popping up everywhere.

Mistral became the best-known member of the Félibrige when he won the Nobel Prize in Literature, which was granted to him "in recognition of the fresh originality and true inspiration of his poetic production, which faithfully reflects the natural scenery and native spirit of his people, and, in addition, his significant work as a Provençal philologist." His most celebrated work, and the one mainly responsible for his Nobel Prize, is his epic poem, *Mirèio* ("Mireille") published in 1859.

So, next time you are in Provence enjoying the rich heritage of the region and you see a dish on the menu with the name "Mireille" in it, or notice a street called "Mistral," or see a sign written in Provençal, you might want to give a thought to Freddie and the Félibrige.

"Chaque année, le rossignol revêt des plumes neuves, mais il garde sa chanson."

("Every year, the nightingale dons new feathers, but he doesn't change his song.")

– Frédéric Mistral

- Mistral used the money from his Nobel Prize to found the *Museon Arlaten* – a museum dedicated to preserving the memory of everyday Provençal life. It's located at 29 rue de la République in Arles.

Mireille

Mireille, or *Mirèio* in Provençal, is Frédéric Mistral's epic poem, which he wrote in Provençal and translated into French. It's also the name of the young heroine of this story.

In *Mireille*, Mistral painted the idealized world of his childhood: a rural Provence filled with folklore and customs passed from generation to generation. He started writing his poetic magnum opus during his early twenties and took between seven and eight years to finish it. *Mireille* was published in 1859, and Charles Gounod turned it into an opera of the same name in 1864.

Here is a short summary of the tragic tale of *Mireille*:

Mireille: The Story

It was the morning of June 24, the festival of Saint Jean. In Arles, the girls who worked on the silkworm farm were filling their aprons with freshly picked mulberry leaves destined to become the worms' breakfast. As they chatted, Taven, a witch who lived in the nearby *Val d'Enfer* (Valley of Hell) joined them and cast a spell which made them all speak their minds freely.

One of the girls revealed that she would only marry for money: nothing but a very rich man would do for her. Mireille, the 15-year-old daughter of the wealthy silkworm farmer, declared that she would marry only for love – even if the one she loved were poor and shy. The others laughed and teased her because they all knew that Mireille had already fallen in love with the poor, barefoot basket-maker named Vincent who came from the other side of the river – the wrong side.

The other girls moved along and Mireille poured out her heart to Taven, telling the witch of her predicament. Her love was forbidden because her father was the rich owner of a silkworm farm, and Vincent's father was poor. Taven sympathized with the downhearted damsel and promised to try and help. As soon as Taven had gone, Vincent showed up and the young couple renewed their vow of undying love. They decided to break the news to their parents and vowed that if their families wouldn't agree to the match, that they would run away and meet up in the church at Saintes-Maries-de-la-Mer.

Later that day, while festivities were underway in front of Arles' ancient Roman arena, Ourrias, a self-confident *gardian* (cowherd), approached Mireille and started flirting. She wasted no time in letting him know that she was not the least bit interested, and he went sulking away.

Then Mireille saw her father (Ramon) and Vincent's father (Ambroise) talking. She tiptoed up to listen to the conversation. Ambroise confided that his son had confessed to being in love with a girl from a rich family and he didn't know what to do. Ramon suggested that giving Vincent a good beating might bring him to his senses.

Horrified by the thought of her beloved being battered, Mireille jumped in to confess that she was the one Vincent loved and that she was madly in love with him as well. Her father flew into a rage and ordered Mireille to go straight home.

Meanwhile, the news spread fast and when Ourrias found out he had been scorned for a lowly basket-maker, it was a blow to his ego. He was determined to win Mireille's heart. He decided to go to the *Val d'Enfer*, that magical place where fairies and sprites lived, to search for Taven. He planned to ask the witch for a love potion that would make Mireille fall in love with him.

On the way, Ourrias met Vincent and was overcome by a jealous fury at the sight of the one who Mireille had chosen over him. Vincent tried to calm the crazed cowherd, but Ourrias whacked him with his trident (the stick with a metal three-pronged tip that *gardians* carry to prod the bulls). He left the young boy for dead and fled the scene. Taven came by and found Vincent.

The next day Vincenette (Vincent's sister) sneaked into Mireille's room and told her that Vincent had been badly hurt by Ourrias. He was still alive and Taven had taken him to Saintes-Maries-de-la-Mer. Mireille decided right then and there to go to her beloved Vincent.

She left in such a hurry that she didn't think to take water with her or even to wear a hat. She walked and ran through the sizzling Camargue heat to get to her true love. But, the sun was beating down so forcefully on her that she succumbed to sunstroke. Even though Mireille was dying, she carried on, determined to reach her beloved Vincent.

In her barely-alive state, Mireille made it to Saintes-Maries-de-la-Mer and stumbled into the church. The pilgrims were singing a heavenly hymn and Mireille caught a glimpse of Vincent. She ran to him and collapsed in his arms. She had just enough time to gaze into his eyes and declare her love for him before she died.

The moral of this tale is that... One should never leave home without one's hat.

This Provençal Romeo and Juliet story contains all the elements of Mistral's treasured Provence: the landscape, festivals, dances, and costumes, as well as the *gardians* and their horses and bulls. And, of course, Mireille herself was the perfect Provençal lass.

Some theorize that Mistral's poem was inspired by a personal experience. They say that young Freddie had also tasted a forbidden love when he fell for a poor girl who was below his station. While there's no direct evidence of this, some researchers do see hints of it in his memoir. Mistral himself denied it, saying that if he had known Mireille, he wouldn't have written *Mireille*, he would have been too busy being Vincent.

Mireille: The Name

Before Mistral's masterpiece was published, there wasn't a girl or woman in all of France who was called Mireille. So how did Mistral come up with this name? It seems that he invented it.

He claimed that, as a boy, he heard the word used to refer to a beautiful young girl: "a lovely mireille" (*mirèio* in Provençal). In his poetic young mind, he imagined that there must have been some long-forgotten heroine called by that name.

After the success of *Mireille*, the poem, and *Mireille*, the opera, people were longing to give their daughters the same name as the beautiful and popular heroine of Provence. But they couldn't: it wasn't on the approved list of baby names.

In France, each day of the year is the name day for a Catholic saint and most children are named after one of them. At one time, these saint names were the only ones accepted on birth certificates, with the exception of a few historic monikers. It was only in 1993 that parents gained the right to name their babies whatever they saw fit – as long as it wasn't detrimental to the child.

So, in 1900, long before the naming laws were changed, when the first Provençal parents wanted to call their little girl Mireille, the priest balked: "Désolé (sorry), but zat name is not on my list."

Mistral ran to the rescue, explaining that Mireille was surely a form of Marie (Mary). Mistral put forth a persuasive argument, and the clergy and State were convinced. Eighty-six little Mireilles had their births registered in France in 1900. Their name day is the same as those with the name Marie: August 15, the day of Assumption of the Virgin Mary.

The name's popularity peaked in 1947, when almost 5,000 new little Mireilles came into the world. But today, it's relatively rare: There were only five Mireilles born in 2011, and one in 2015.

Costume of Arles

No discussion of the customs of Provence would be complete without a peek at some of Provence's distinctive costumes. In southwest Provence, especially in the Arles area, traditional dress is very important. It's worn for cultural events and special occasions, and there's even a costume festival every summer.

A few centuries ago, most regions had their own particular style of dress which evolved and adapted through the years. But at the end of the nineteenth century, old ways and old styles of clothing were giving way to a more modern, Paris-inspired fashion.

As you might guess, Frédéric Mistral and the Félibrige had a hand in keeping traditional costume alive. They took a snapshot, as it were, of the nineteenth-century dress and declared it to be the traditional Provençal costume.

In the story of *Mireille*, Mistral described in detail the clothing worn by his 15-year-old heroine. In fact, the costume for young ladies is now known as the costume of Mireille. Not only did Mistral portray the clothing in his poetry, but he also published an article in 1884 about the

Arlésienne costume and its importance as a symbol, even calling it the jewel of Provence culture.

The costume became standardized, and today there are four basic outfits for the ladies of Arles. They differ according to age, and are named after their headwear, since the dresses are similar.

The costume "de bonnet" (of the bonnet) is usually worn by girls under 8 years old so they don't have to worry about fiddling with their hair.

The costume *"en cravat"* or *"de Mireille"* (costume of Mireille) is worn from approximately the age of 8 to 15 years old. The *cravat* is a triangle of white fabric tied in "rabbit ears" leaving two ends sticking up at the front of the head. This is what Mireille wore in Mistral's poem.

The costume *"en ruban"* or *"d'Arlésienne"* (costume of the woman from Arles) is usually worn after the age of 15. This ensemble is worn with the *ruban* (ribbon). The upswept hair is gathered in a white muslin cloth and then a wide ribbon is wrapped around it which extends at the back of the head. The dress is of finer fabric than the "Mireille" and loses its apron.

The costume *"gansé"* is a more fanciful version of the *Arlésienne* which is worn for weddings and other special ceremonies. Instead of ribbon, lace cloth is wrapped around the hair leaving large "rabbit ears" in the front. It's usually worn with a lace shawl.

The elaborate upswept hairstyle topped by the headwear is an indispensable part of the ensemble which means that women with short hair are left out of the costume festival.

- Note: Here we are talking about the costume of Arles. There are other costumes in other areas of Provence.

Costume & Headwear of Arles

Costume "de bonnet"

Costume "en ruban"

Costume "gansé"

Costume "en cravat" or "de Mireille"

Virgin Ceremony

To give the costume even more importance, Mistral invented a special ceremony. In 1903, he created the *Festo Vierginenco* (*Fête des Vierges* in French or "Virgin Festival" in English). It was designed as a coming-of-age party for young Provençal ladies who were graduating from their *Mireille* outfits to their adult *Arlésienne* ensembles. They would be presented with a diploma and they would promise to wear their traditional garments proudly, to share their cultural knowledge with other young girls, and to make sure the costume tradition continued. Mistral started this ceremony in Arles and hoped that each village would take up the tradition. Today, however, only Saintes-Maries-de-la-Mer continues to uphold this tradition.

The Queen of Arles

Another way that Arles keeps the costume tradition alive is by electing a queen every three years. The candidates are tested in history, literature, architecture, arts, traditions of the region, and the Provençal language. The queen is the ambassador for local traditions, and she's present at all cultural events and many public occasions. At these events, she always wears her *Arlésienne* costume. The first queen was elected in 1930 on the occasion of the 100th anniversary of Frédéric Mistral's birth.

Men's Costume

The men have a costume too, but it isn't nearly as showy as the ladies'. It is very simple, consisting of a long-sleeved shirt, trousers, waistcoat, and wide-brimmed hat.

- **The Costume Festival** (*Fête du Costume*) is held the first Sunday in July in Arles.

Provençal Nativity Play

La Pastorale

The *pastorale* is one of the many traditions that fills the Christmas season. It's a Nativity play that incorporates a nineteenth-century Provençal village into the story. *Pastorales* are often performed in the Provençal language, but some are in French. The word *pastorale* basically means "shepherd's song" and is a reference to the Biblical Christmas story where the shepherds are the first to hear the good news.

Early versions of these performances only told the Biblical narrative of the birth of Jesus, but in the mid 1800s, Antoine Maurel, a Provençal poet, added some local flavor to the Christmas tale. His *pastorale* was one of the first to incorporate the people of the Provençal villages and to add a bit of Provençal humor. Other *pastorales* exist and at least two were written by members of the Félibrige, but Maurel's *pastorale* is still one of the most popular.

This is a simplified version of Maurel's pastorale which was first performed in 1844. (Note – it's not a politically correct play.)

Maurel Pastorale

It's night and shepherds are in the hills tending their sheep. Suddenly a bright light appears above them. It's an angel who announces that Jesus has been born in Bethlehem (which, conveniently, happens to be a Provençal village). The shepherds decide to go welcome the Holy Infant.

As they travel, they stop at every home along the way to wake the inhabitants and tell them the good news. A tambourine player and a drummer join in, reducing the chance that anyone will sleep through this event. One by one, house by house, people hear the news, grab a gift (something associated with their profession), and join the parade.

They come across the *aveugle* (blind man). He's blind because his oldest son was kidnapped by the Gypsies and he cried so much he lost his sight. His youngest son leads him along in the procession.

As they make their way to Bethlehem, Provence, others join this motley crew. The *meunier* (miller) fills a sack of flour for the Holy Child and then he and his donkey join them. Pimpara, the *rémouleur* (knife and scissor sharpener) who likes to drink a bit too much follows along as well. Then they come across two friends who are not the brightest lights on the Christmas tree: Jiget, the *bègue* (stutterer) and Pistachié, the *peureux* (fearful). These two have been hoodwinked by the Gypsies into paying a sack full of silver to buy their own shadows.

When the shepherds and their followers arrive in the Provençal Bethlehem, they stop at the house of Roustido, an older man. When he hears the news, he goes to tell his friend, Jourdan. The two old men make such a ruckus that they wake Margarido, Jourdan's cantankerous wife, who is sleeping upstairs. She joins the two men, and the three of them leave for the stable, arguing and spreading the news all along the way.

Everyone stops outside Benvengu's house. He is Jourdan's son-in-law and the owner of a large farm. He's known for always welcoming company with a few glasses of wine and the thirsty travelers are sure the Baby Jesus won't mind if they stop for just a few minutes to refresh themselves. After everyone has rested and put back a few drinks, they continue their journey.

When they arrive at the stable where the Holy Infant was born, they all present him with their gifts and many miracles occur: Margarido and Jourdan start to get along, and they even hold hands and kiss. Jiget the stutterer loses his stutter. The Gypsies feel ashamed of themselves and give the blind man's son back to him. Miraculously, his eyesight is restored and everyone goes on their way rejoicing.

There are several different *pastorale* plays with different characters, but the idea is pretty much the same. They tell the stories of the townspeople making their way to see the newborn baby in Bethlehem, Provence. And since different *pastorales* feature different characters, everyone in the town is represented.

These Christmas plays go hand in hand with the Provence *santons*, those little figurines that populate the Provençal crèche. Every miniature figure has its own story which is told in one of the Christmas *pastorales*. For more about *santons* and other Provence traditions, see my book *French Holidays & Traditions*.

PART 5:
WILD WEST OF
PROVENCE

There are men on horseback wearing wide-brimmed hats and driving herds of horned cattle across the plains. But this isn't the American West, it's southern France. The Camargue in the southwest corner of Provence is very different from the rest of the region and is often compared to the American Wild West. However, the Provence cowboys, or *gardians* as they're called, feel more of an affinity with the American Indians than their counterpart, the American cowboys.

Marquis, Cowboy, or Indian?

In September 1906, a 37-year-old Marquis from Provence was standing on the dock in Ghent, Belgium, bidding farewell to a group of Native Americans who had become his dear friends. The Indians, as they were called in those days, were boarding a ship headed back to America after more than a year of traveling through France and other parts of Europe with Buffalo Bill's Wild West show. As they stepped onto the boat, they threw a package at the feet of the Marquis, their French brother, to whom they had given the name Faithful Bird. He tore open the parcel and found an Indian chief costume with a long, feathered headdress. A tear rolled down his cheek.

Who was this "Faithful Bird"? He was also known as the Marquis Falco de Baroncelli-Javon, and this is his story. His aristocratic ancestors had moved from Florence, Italy to Provence in the fifteenth century, and although they still had their titles, the family was no longer wealthy. They lived a modest lifestyle and even spoke Provençal, the language of the common people.

The Marquis Becomes a Cowboy

When Baroncelli was in his late teens, he fell under the influence of the much older Frédéric Mistral and the Félibrige. By this time, the Félibrige had been using their poetry to preserve and renew Provençal traditions for about 30 years.

The young Baroncelli wanted to do his part too, but he was more drawn to horses and cattle than to poetry. In 1895, at the age of 26, he married and moved to a rented *manade* (ranch) in the Camargue where he became a *gardian* – a Provençal cowboy. The Marquis-cowboy soon decided this was where he would make his mark. He would revive the customs of the noble *gardians* who tended the horses and rounded up the cattle in the Camargue, this marshy area of Provence.

Following Mistral's lead, he took a bit of poetic license as he began standardizing, refining, and adding to the traditions of the Provence cowboy. When he needed inspiration, he turned to the French Western novels which were popular at the time. They told tales of an American West which was much more idyllic than realistic. So, with his head full of romantic notions, the Marquis-cowboy set about creating the perfect "Wild West of Provence."

The Marquis-Cowboy Meets The Wild West

In the spring of 1905, the Marquis couldn't believe his ears when he heard that the American Wild West was coming to France. William Cody, better known as Buffalo Bill, was going to spend most of the year traveling around France with his Wild West show.

The timing was perfect. Just a year earlier, Baroncelli had founded the *Nacioun Gardiano* (Gardian Nation) to organize all the cowboys in Provence. He had designed costumes for them, and standardized their horse and bull games. He was certain that Buffalo Bill would be eager to see the horsemanship skills of his Camargue *gardians* and maybe even use them in his show. He wrote to the showman to offer their services, but received no response.

Undeterred, Baroncelli decided to take the train to Paris and see the production for himself. Maybe he would even get a chance to talk to Bill about featuring his *gardians* in the act. When the Marquis-cowboy from Provence arrived, however, he was overwhelmed by the vastness and diversity of the Wild West encampment: 800 people, 500 horses, a small herd of buffalo, and an entire teepee village traveled with the show. They had come across the Atlantic on three ships and it would take three trains to move them between the 120 cities they would visit in France.

As Baroncelli watched the grand performance, he was dumbfounded by the horsemanship that he saw during the *Rough Riders of the World* segment. American cowboys and Indians performed alongside Turks, Arabs, Mongols, and Georgians. They all wore their traditional costumes, rode their distinctive horses, and exhibited breathtaking riding skills that the Marquis could not have imagined: even doing acrobatics atop a galloping horse and other rodeo-type stunts.

Baroncelli thought of his *gardians* back in the Camargue. He had considered them quite the show-stoppers, when they performed their one traditional game. That's right, they only had one: galloping toward a post with a small ring secured to it and trying to spear the ring with their lance. Their performance now seemed very humble by comparison. He left Paris determined to make true showmen out of his Provençal cowboys.

As soon as he arrived back in Provence, he went straight to Avignon to search through the archives in the Pope's Palace. He was confident he would uncover some long-lost *gardian* games that had been performed hundreds of years earlier. And he did... Or so he said...

He introduced the newly-discovered horse games, which he claimed had been performed in medieval times, to an appreciative crowd. However, when the conservationist at the Pope's Palace denied that there was any record of these "long-lost" games, Baroncelli had to fess up. While it would have been ideal to have resurrected ancient Provençal traditions, the truth was that he needed some new games for his *gardian* performances, and since he couldn't find any, he had simply made some up. But what did it matter? All traditions are created at some time or another. Anyway, everyone enjoyed the new games and no one really cared if they were old or new.

The Marquis-Cowboy Becomes an Indian

In addition to ideas for new horse games, the Marquis had come away from the Wild West show with the feeling that he and his *gardians* were more Indian than cowboy. He was firmly convinced that there was a link between the Native Americans and the Camargue *gardians*. He identified with the Indians' way of living with nature, their strong traditions, and their struggle against the oppressor. In the United States, the government was trying to change the Indians' way of life and make them live like "white men." In France, Baroncelli and the Félibrige were trying to keep the State from taking away their traditions and language, and making them identical to the folks in Paris. Perhaps the Native Americans that the Marquis befriended through the Wild West show felt a connection as well. They gave him the name Zinktala Waste or Faithful Bird. The Faithful Bird, in turn, gave Indian nicknames to all his *gardians*.

While Baroncelli was back at the ranch renaming his *gardians* and teaching them the new games he had created, the Wild West show continued to work its way through France. In October 1905, the Wild West trains rolled into the south, and the Marquis-Indian was there to meet them, attending shows in Toulouse, Nimes, and Avignon.

Baroncelli must have been quivering with excitement in December 1905, when two Dakota Sioux chiefs accepted the invitation to come to his ranch. The Indians were treated to a demonstration of the *gardians* selecting and herding bulls. When the visit was over and the Indians were riding away in their carriage, *gardians* on their white horses formed an escort. In a final salute to Faithful Bird, the two chiefs stood up, put their hands on their hearts, and sang their war song, *Liberator's Chant*, as they disappeared around the corner in a cloud of Camargue dust.

As the winter of 1905 closed in, Baroncelli had the chance to nurture his friendship with another Indian, Jacob White Eyes from the Oglala tribe. Buffalo Bill had parked his Wild West equipment and animals in Marseille and gone back to America for the winter. Jacob White Eyes was one of the men who stayed behind to tend the animals. The Marquis paid several visits to him during the winter and a lasting friendship was born. When springtime came, the show packed up and began its 1906 European tour, and Jacob White Eyes sent postcards to the Marquis from all the European cities where they performed.

The friendship between Faithful Bird and Jacob White Eyes continued by letter for many years after the Wild West show left European shores. In a 1906 letter to Jacob White Eyes, the Marquis expressed his deep feelings for the Native Americans. He related how he had the impression that he had been an Indian in a previous life, and that he felt he had finally found his long-lost brothers.

Baroncelli had been profoundly affected by his meeting with the American Indians and by the things he saw in the Wild West show. Neither he nor his *gardians* nor the Camargue would ever be the same. So, in September 1906, when the Wild West show had completed its European tour and was preparing to head home for good, the

Marquis went to Ghent, Belgium to say goodbye. Faithful Bird, the Provençal Marquis who had become a cowboy then an Indian, stood on the dock watching the ship slide out to sea. He pulled the headdress out of the package and slipped it on his head. As the feathers trailed down his back, he raised his hand in farewell to his American Indian brothers.

So long, my brothers. Faithful Bird will never forget you... In fact, I think I'll name my ranch hands after you.

- **Did Buffalo Bill Leave French Toast Behind?** Frédéric Mistral had a little dog which he called Pan Pardu (*Pain Perdu* in French and "French Toast" in English). He claimed the pup had once belonged to Buffalo Bill, but while the Wild West show was traveling through Provence, little French Toast got lost. He wandered around looking everywhere for his owner. One day, he trotted into the town of Maillane and saw Frédéric Mistral, who had a striking resemblance to Buffalo Bill: they both had longish hair, long goatees and wore wide-brimmed hats. French Toast thought he had found his master, and Mistral gladly adopted him.

More from the
Marquis

The Provençal Marquis who had a soft spot for the American Indians was always looking to help the disadvantaged or take on a worthy cause. Not only did he organize the *gardians* and give them a sense of pride in their profession, but he was also influential in many other aspects of Camargue culture:

- Gypsy Pilgrimage – It was Baroncelli who persuaded the Church to allow the Gypsies to participate in the services in Saintes-Maries-de-la-Mer during their annual pilgrimage. See *Saints and Gypsies*.
- Camargue National Park – He helped to transform the Camargue from desolate land to an organized natural park which continues to attract tourism to the area. He campaigned against the plan to drain the swamps which are home to many species of birds.
- Gardian Nation – He created the Gardian Nation. The organization's stated goal is to "preserve and

glorify the dress, customs, and traditions of the region of Arles, of the Camargue and of the bull country, to help the language flourish and spread the Félibrige doctrine found in the poetic works of Frédéric Mistral and his disciples..."

- Camargue Cross – He asked Hermann Paul to design the *croix camarguaise* (Camargue cross) which is the symbol of the Gardian Nation.
- Bull Games – He standardized the bull games.
- Stock Breeding – He also worked with the black Camargue bulls and the white horses to breed them back to their original state which had been diluted through cross-breeding.
- Western Films – Jean Hamman was one of the first people Baroncelli met at the Wild West show. Hamman was an early French Western film maker, and after he met Baroncelli, he would use the Marquis' Camargue ranch to shoot his films.

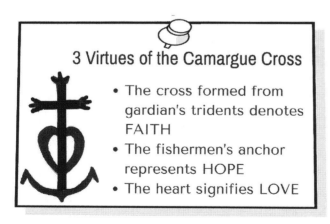

3 Virtues of the Camargue Cross

- The cross formed from gardian's tridents denotes FAITH
- The fishermen's anchor represents HOPE
- The heart signifies LOVE

By 1930 the Marquis, who had spent all his money making the Camargue a better place, was broke. He had to move out of his rented *mas* (farmhouse). The people of Saintes-

Maries-de-la-Mer were so fond of their benefactor that they gave him some property to build another *mas* on. It was called the Mas du Simbèu. The *simbèu* is an old bull that wears a bell and is the leader of the herd: a very fitting metaphor for the Marquis, the leader of the Gardian Nation.

During World War II German troops requisitioned and occupied Baroncelli's beloved Mas du Simbèu, and he went to live with his daughter. In December 1943 the Marquis died, leaving instructions that he wanted to be buried on the land of Mas du Simbèu, which at the time was still occupied by the Nazis. When the German troops left a year later, they blew up the Marquis' *mas*.

Baroncelli's heart had been placed in the chapel of the Palais du Roure in Avignon alongside his ancestors, and his body had been cremated. In 1950, seven years after his death, a tomb was built on the site where the Mas du Simbèu had once stood, and the Marquis' ashes were placed inside. Legend has it that as the procession carried his remains along the road to their final resting place, the bulls in the bordering pastures walked slowly along beside them. Just as if they were following their master one last time.

What to See and Do

- Palais du Roure – The Baroncelli family home and small museum can be visited in Avignon.
- Baroncelli is celebrated every year at the time of the Gypsy pilgrimage in Saintes-Maries-de-la-Mer. The day after all the religious services have finished is dedicated to the man who made it all possible.

Bull Games

Take Me Out to the Bull Game

Southwest Provence, around Arles and the Camargue, is the land of the *taureau* (bull). People there have been playing and fighting with those horned beasts for centuries. Today, many variations of "bull games" exist, but there are two main types: the Spanish-style *corrida* and the Provence-style *course Camarguaise*. Each one involves a different kind of bull and each has a very different outcome for the animal.

The Corrida
Spanish-Style Bullfight
The Bull Dies

The earliest record of a blood sport bull game in Provence is from 1402, when one was held in Arles in honor of the Count of Provence. These early "games" were violent and bloody, often pitting other animals, such as lions or bears, against the bulls. They evolved into the Spanish-style bullfights that we know today where a matador faces, and usually kills, the bull.

This type of bullfight is called a *corrida*, and, even though it is controversial, it is still alive and well in this part of France. Only Spanish bulls participate in the *corrida* because they are larger and more aggressive than the Camargue bulls. The *corrida* rarely ends well for these animals.

Course Camarguaise
The Bull Lives

As early as the end of the 1800s, the *corrida* was being criticized for its violence, and its popularity began to wane. So, a kinder, gentler "bull game" was invented, which we know today as the *course Camarguaise*. In this game, only quick-moving young men are in the arena with the bull. And instead of killing him, they try to remove objects tied to his horns. A very informal survey has shown that nine out of ten bulls prefer this type of game. And we are pretty sure the tenth one didn't understand the question.

Only Camargue bulls get to participate in the *course Camarguaise*. They are smaller and a bit less aggressive than their Spanish cousins, but they are still plenty dangerous. The black bulls are definitely the stars of the show. They get top billing on the programs and the best-known bulls really pull in the crowds.

Bull games are popular entertainment in this region, and most towns have their own arena. In the summer, one of these bull events is held almost daily someplace or another.

How the Course Camarguaise Works

There are three main players in this game:

1. *Cocardier* – The bull wearing the items tied to his horns is called the *cocardier*. In the early days of these games, these objects might have been flowers, scarves, or even sausages. Now they are standardized and are called *attributes*. They consist of:

- *Cocarde*: a small bow between the horns.
- *Glands*: two tassels – one at the base of each horn.
- *Ficelles*: strings wound around the base of each horn.

2. *Raseteurs* – Young men dressed in white who try to snatch the bull's attributes. They attempt to pluck as many objects from the bull's horns as possible – without being harmed by the unfriendly bovine, who wants to keep his attributes. They wear a special hook, called a *crochet*, attached to their hand to help them grab the goods.

3. *Tourneurs* – These are also young men dressed in white. Normally, they are a bit older and are former *raseteurs*. Their job is to get the bull into position for the *raseteurs* to make their move.

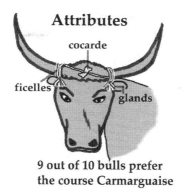

Attributes

cocarde

ficelles

glands

**9 out of 10 bulls prefer
the course Carmarguaise**

But before the game begins, there is usually a bit of pageantry. It often starts with a marching band, followed by women in Arlesienne costume, then the *raseteurs* and *tourneurs* make their way around the arena.

When it's time for the action to begin, all the people clear out of the bullring and make way for the bull. He's let in and left alone for a few minutes to acclimatize to his surroundings. He's usually not very happy to find himself in the ring surrounded by a crowd of people, so he paws the ground, snorts, and bellows at the crowd.

After the bull's alone time, the *raseteurs* and *tourneurs*, join him in the arena. They work in pairs: the *tourneur* waves and calls out to the *taureau* to get him into a good position for his *raseteur* partner, who then runs across the arena at an angle. The bull turns to chase him and when they meet (hopefully near the barrier) the *raseteur* tries to grab one of the attributes tied to the animal's horns and jumps over the barrier. The enraged bull usually stops at the barrier, but sometimes he rams it with his horns, and sometimes he even jumps over it right behind the *raseteur*. This is why the *raseteurs* jump up on a high wall and stay there for a bit to see whether the bull is following them. This dangerous dance goes on for 15 minutes, or until all the attributes are picked off the bull.

After the *taureau*'s 15 minutes of fame, he leaves the arena, probably out of breath, but unharmed.

Even More Bull Events

The people of this region are crazy for their bulls, and while the *course Camarguaise* and the Corrida are the main events, they are, by no means, the only ones.

Abrivado & Bandido

When there is a big bull event in the arena, there is often an *abrivado* beforehand. This is when the *gardians* on their white horses round up bulls from the *manade* (ranch) and herd them to the arena – right through the town's streets! On these days, you will see warning signs posted advising people not to park their cars on the roadside. After the arena event, there is a *bandido*, which is the same thing in reverse. The bulls are herded back to their pasture.

During the *abrivado* and *bandido* the bulls are completely surrounded by the *gardians* and their horses. These Provence cowboys display their herding skills by keeping the bulls contained and under control. Some of the spectators (mostly foolhardy young men) take it upon themselves to try to help the bulls break free. They might do this by jumping onto the horses' necks or otherwise trying to distract horse and rider. If a bull does manage to escape, the *gardians* quickly round it back up. And all this happens at high speed on the city streets.

Encierro

An *encierro* is another way of getting the bulls to and from the arena. In an *encierro*, the streets of the town are lined with barriers and the bulls are let loose to run through the streets. Some "brave" folk run along with them.

Taureau Piscine

Another event worth mentioning is *taureau piscine* ("bull swimming pool"). In this circus-like event, a plastic wading pool is set up in the arena and young cows participate instead of bulls. The cows do have horns, although they are padded on the ends, but they are not as ferocious as bulls. Normally, the goal is to get the cow into the pool.

So, whether you want to see bulls wearing ribbons or cows in swimming pools, this area of Provence surely has a bovine event to suit your taste.

Find a Bull Event Near You

You can find out when the bull events are taking place by asking at the Tourist Office, or you can look at the Féderation Française de la Course Camarguaise website: ffcc.info

Terminology Recap

Attributes: Items tied to bull's horns
Abrivado: When the bulls are herded to the arena.
Bandido: When the bulls are returning from the arena.
Corrida: The bull is killed.
Course Camarguaise: The bull is not killed.
Gardians/Gardianes: Cowboys/cowgirls.
Raseteur: Young man who tries to take attributes from the bull's horns.
Tauromachie: A general term for bull games, but normally associated with the *corrida*.

Vovo
The Little Bull with a
Big Chip on His Shoulder

In the *course Camarguaise*, it's the bulls who are the true stars of the show. Their names headline the posters, and some of the more extraordinary beasts even have commemorative statues erected in their honor. Such is the case for Vovo.

This is the story of one bull who became a celebrity of the *course Camarguaise*. He was called Vovo the Magnificent, Vovo the Terrible, The Cannonball, The Black Meteor... And he was a little bull with a big chip on his shoulder.

Vovo's story begins in August 1943. Some *gardians* were rounding up bulls for an *abrivado* and they took a few cows along as encouragement for the bulls to join them. There was a bit of confusion when one of the horses was startled, and when the dust settled and everything was back under control, they saw that one of the cows had escaped. When the rancher realized it was Gyptis, he told the *gardians* not to worry about her. He knew she would come back to the ranch on her own.

But Gyptis found that she liked going solo. She contentedly wandered through the Camargue for more than six months. Then one day, she was grazing beside a pasture when she got a glimpse of Prouvenço, the most handsome bull she had ever seen. Her head swooned. It was love at first sight. The couple had a few wonderful evenings together, and about nine months later, little Vovo was born.

Gyptis gave birth in November 1944 and she and her baby were managing just fine on their own. But when the owner of the property where Gyptis had set up her little home discovered them, he called Gyptis' owner. A few months later, mother and son were returned to Mom's original ranch. But Vovo never forgot the wild place where he was born and he often ran away and made his way back there.

In 1946, at two years of age, Vovo was scheduled to make his public debut in the bullring. But the young bull had other ideas. As he and the others were being herded to the arena holding area – and just before the huge doors were closed – Vovo did a U-turn and ran right back out. He had somewhere else to go. But the *gardians* caught up with him just outside of town, turned him around, and headed him back toward the arena.

As soon as they entered the village, Vovo spotted a photographer taking photos of something else and not paying attention to the approaching bull. He charged the poor man and sent him flying. Then he ran away again.

When the feisty young bull did finally have his turn in the arena, he showed his violent temper and his disdain for men. The crowd loved him and called him the Black Meteor but he also struck fear into their hearts. During his career, Vovo sent many a *raseteur* to the hospital and was the cause of destruction in several arenas.

The bullrings have an open area in the center surrounded by a wooden barrier. Then a few feet further back, there is a higher wall which holds up the spectator seating. Between these two walls, there's a sort of alleyway around the arena. It's not uncommon for bulls to jump over this first barrier in pursuit of the man in white, which is why the *raseteurs* normally jump onto the higher wall. Vovo would often jumped over the barrier – but he was also likely to attack and destroy it.

He's remembered especially for his exploits in 1951 at a *course Carmarguaise* in Lunel. He was in a particularly bad mood that day. He caught up with one unfortunate *raseteur* just before he reached the barrier. Vovo tried to skewer him, then began trampling him. The angry bull even bit a chunk out of the man's scalp. The *raseteur* would surely have been killed if the other *raseteurs* hadn't pulled him out underneath the barrier from the other side. When Vovo saw that his prey had escaped, he was even more infuriated. He began to attack the metal posts supporting the stands, sending the crowd into a panic. When Vovo the Terrible left the ring that day, 48 beams and planks had to be replaced.

He was strong, fast, and full of rage. The crowds loved him. When Vovo was on the bill, the stands would fill up by noon for a 4 o'clock event. But all of that tearing up of arenas took a toll on him physically.

In November 1959, Vovo was 15 years old, just middle-age for a Camargue bull, but his body had been broken and abused by his rage and attacks on boards and beams. He reaped the rewards of his violent temper and died alone in a Camargue pasture located near the tomb of the Marquis de Baroncelli who had passed from this life just before Vovo was born.

Between his fits of anger in the arena, Vovo took the time to sire many sons who would themselves become stars of the *course Camarguaise*. His career was short but eventful. Vovo became a legend and a standard by which the qualities of bulls have been measured ever since.

In 2010, a sculpture of Vovo the Magnificent was erected near the arena in Saintes-Maries-de-la-Mer. In keeping with his uncontrollable character, he's shown crashing through a barrier.

Mom said I needed to go to anger management classes - but that just made me mad !

-VOVO THE MAGNIFICENT-
-VOVO THE TERRIBLE-
-THE BLACK METEOR-
-THE CANNONBALL-

Horses, Bulls, and Gardians

The Camargue

Since the marshy area around Arles and the Camargue isn't suitable for development, it has been of little interest to humans over the years. Thus, it made a perfect home for herds of wild white horses, black cattle, and a multitude of birds, including pink flamingos (and sometimes mosquitos the size of birds).

White Horses

Even though the origins of the Camargue horse are uncertain, it's considered to be one of the oldest breeds in the world. Many compare it to the short, stocky, prehistoric steed painted on the walls of the Lascaux caves in the Dordogne region of France. Could the modern Camargue horse be the descendant of the one that lived alongside those cave people?

Whatever the origins of this horse, it's a mysterious creature. For one thing, it changes color. The colts are brown when they're born, and when they are four or five years old, they turn white – well, actually, light gray, but that's close enough.

These amazing horses once roamed free, but now they live a semi-wild existence. Some of them carry *gardians* and work with bulls, and others carry tourists. They all belong to someone and are fenced in, but there are usually no barns or stables. They sleep in the fields, eat whatever is growing there, and they deal with reproduction on their own.

At one year, the colts are branded and separated from their mother, then at three, they start being tamed and trained. The males are taught to work with bulls, and the females are raised for breeding.

Grandpa at Lascaux

Do you think I look like Grandad ?

Black Bulls

The fearsome Camargue bull is short and thin with a black coat and horns in the shape of a lyre. He's intelligent, agile, and long-lived, reaching 30 to 40 years of age. Like the horse, he lives a semi-wild existence on the Camargue ranches. Bulls are raised mainly for the bull games that are very popular in these parts, and cows are kept for breeding. A few of them, however, do end up as steak.

Gardians

The *gardians* are basically Provençal cowboys who ride the white horses and round up the black bulls. They show off their riding and herding skills at events held throughout the year.

Of course, there is a legend about these three beings and how they came to cohabit in the Camargue marshlands...

Poseidon in the Camargue
A Legend

One day Poseidon, the great god of the sea, was surveying his kingdom from the shores of the Camargue. As he was riding along in his majestic chariot pulled by nine powerful white horses, he spotted a human in the water. The mighty Poseidon approached and slammed down his trident, causing the earth (and the man) to tremble.

"What are you doing here in my domain?" Poseidon demanded.

"I live in this land," the frightened man explained as he made his way to the shore. "This beautiful region is my home, but I have a terrible problem. There is a fearsome animal that also lives here. It's a huge black bull with horns shaped like a lyre. This bull is always chasing me and the only way I can get away from him is to run into the sea."

Poseidon, who had a fondness for the frail human race, decided to help this poor, desperate man. He unhooked the lead horse from his chariot and offered it to the astonished human. "This magnificent horse will help you subdue the black beast," he said. "He will always be your friend, but never your slave. You must allow him to live free and smell the sea, from which he was born."

The man graciously thanked Poseidon and spent the next three days and nights with the high-spirited horse that had never been around a human. Every day the white steed became tamer. Finally, the man was able to climb onto the horse's back, and as soon as he did, the horse took off galloping in the direction of the big black bull.

The poor human was shocked and more than a bit apprehensive. But remembering the trident that Poseidon carried, he broke a three-pronged branch off a tree as they galloped past, and used it to subdue the black beast. From that day on, the man on his horse ruled over the horned tormentor. And that is why, even today, in the Camargue, you can see the *gardians* on their white horses carrying their tridents to control those black bulls.

PROVENCE

PROVENCE

P urple fields and blood-red hills,

R ounds of cicada chants,

O nce a place of saints and dragons,

V agabond gypsies dance,

E ver-boastful Tartarin,

N ostradamus in a trance,

C ustoms of old reverberate

E choes of southern France.

Index of Places

About Margo

I'm American by birth, but now divide my time between London, England and Nice, France (with a sprinkling of other places thrown in for good measure). I enjoy the fact that life in a foreign country is never dull and every day is a new learning experience.

I describe myself as a perpetual student because I'm always taking some kind of course or researching a moment in history that has caught my fancy. I'm curious by nature and always want to know who, what, why, when, where, and how...

I share my adventures (and my questions) with Jeff, my husband of many years. I enjoy travel, history, observing cultures and traditions – and then writing about them, of course.

My other books:

- *French Holidays & Traditions*
- *Curious Histories of Nice, France*

Please visit my website: curiousrambler.com (Curious Rambler)

Other Books

Curious Histories of Nice, France

Find out why Queen Victoria rode around Nice in a donkey cart, how the local specialty may have started out as ammunition, why a cannon announces lunch, and much more... This book tells the intriguing stories of the people and events that have shaped Nice.

French Holidays & Traditions

Do you want to know what paper fish have to do with the first of April? Why the French hand out poisonous flowers on the first of May? What mice have to do with children's teeth? This short book delves into these and other curious French traditions.

Made in the USA
Monee, IL
03 November 2019

16278944R10087